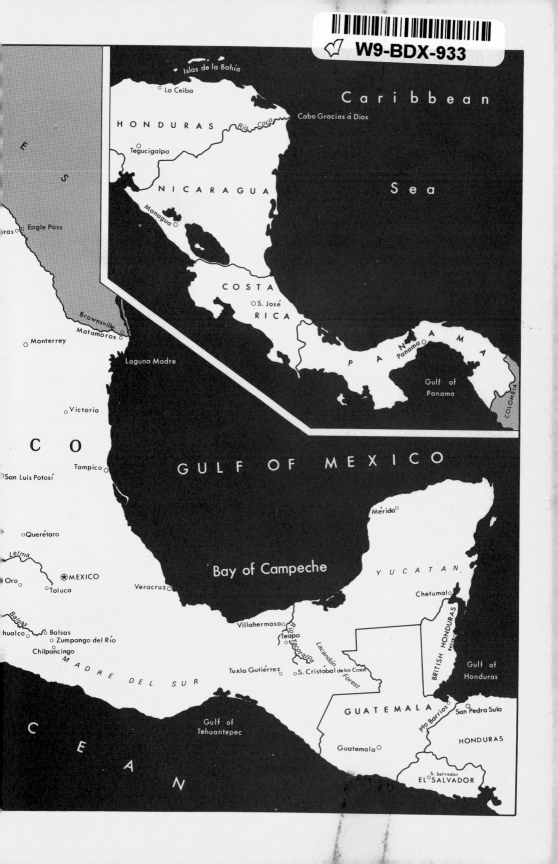

EL LOBO
AND
SPANISH
GOLD

EL LOBO
AND
SPANISH
GOLD

A Texas Maverick in Mexico

By C. E. (Rick) Ricketts

FOREWORD BY ARIS A. (BOB) MALLAS

DRAWINGS BY DAVE MANUEL

MADRONA PRESS, INC. / AUSTIN, TEXAS

TO RICARDO

AND ALL THE OTHER TYPICAL TROPICAL TRAMPS AND *gambusinos* WITH WHOM I HAVE SHARED MANY MEMORABLE, AND SOME DANGEROUS, EXPERIENCES.

Foreword

IT WAS DAWN IN THE VALLEY and the haze hung in light, airy patches over our camp. The fire was beginning to blaze up as the Indian cook carefully fed it dry grasses, then small twigs, and finally small limbs. With the snap of the fire and the gradual coming of light, the Indian miners stirred themselves one by one. Throwing wool serapes over their shoulders, they squatted before the small fire to warm their hands.

Over the fire was the ever-present kettle of beans, and in the coals a huge coffee pot began to bubble. The cook leaned over and scraped some coals to the side and placed over them a large iron skillet filled with grease. As the grease began to snap and pop, the cook dropped potato chunks—skins and all—into the skillet. Corn tortillas, made up the night before, were warming on a piece of tin, placed near the fire to reflect the heat. Wood was scarce here in the valley and the Indians had learned long ago to use it sparingly.

The morning was cold and the moist haze added to the chill, but the Indians knew that the cool dampness would disappear when the sun rose. By midafternoon the temperature would reach 120 degrees, and the valley would be bril-

liantly clear, but with ever-changing patterns of light and
shadow as the sun advanced. This was as certain as the rainy
season, which was yet two moons away.

Soon the breakfast of beans, potatoes, tortillas, and coffee
was ready. There was a grace and dignity in the eating ritual,
as each took his turn at filling a tin plate, then squatted to eat
in leisurely fashion, talking softly to others near him.

The Indian miners were short and lean and seemed to move
with the grace and swiftness of a cat. Each was dressed in
baggy white trousers and shirt, with a hand-loomed virgin
wool serape over his shoulder, and wore a white straw hat,
much stained with sweat. While the clothing was shabby and
worn, it was clean, as were hair, face, and hands. The work
these men did each day was dirty, but they bathed frequently
in the river, with much splashing and laughing, like a group
of boys.

The Indians ranged in age from eighteen to thirty-five,
though it was hard to tell their ages. There was a certain
sameness in their faces — an interesting quality that con-
veyed a look of shyness, yet good humor. Basically a happy
people, they enjoyed their hard life and made the most of it.
Hostility and distrust showed only when a Mexican appeared
in the camp. The hostility stemmed from many years of ex-
ploitation, causing the natives to avoid contact with Mexicans
as much as possible. Yet their animosity and suspicion did not
extend to the "gringo" geologists in the camp, who had won
their trust, affection, and respect.

With the growing light, the haze lifted with a rush of cool
air, revealing the spectacular scenery of the valley. The camp
was in the shadow of a sheer cliff, rising more than 4,000
feet. Almost 50 feet below the camp was the Urique River,
shallow and sluggish in the dry season. Within two months
it would become a rushing torrent, extending almost to the
campsite. Across the valley, about 100 yards, a steep mountain

towered more than 5,000 feet, and behind it another 3,000 feet higher, then still another rising to 9,500 feet above sea level. Where the sunlight struck the mountain fully, it cast upon it a purple mantle, a reflection off the waist-high grasses. Since the camp was 8,000 feet below the plateau, some part of it was in shadow at all times, and evening came early.

As the haze lifted, thousands of green parrots in flocks of 100 to 150 flew up the valley, each one screeching constantly. The screeching stopped only when they reached a point across from the camp, almost halfway up the mountain, where the sparse trees on the hillside produced a bean-like pod. The parrots tore the pods apart with greedy squawks.

The noise of the parrots was the signal for the two gringo geologists to wake up, and in a few minutes they came to the fire from the little grass and mud hut the Indians had built thirty feet up the trail. The cook dished their breakfast—first a cup of steaming black coffee, then the beans, potatoes, and tortillas. As they ate, the other Indians disappeared into the surrounding area, busy with their personal chores, but not a sound came back to the camp. The geologists ate quickly, discussing the work detail for the day, and suddenly, as if by magic, the Indians reappeared, ready for work. No one had to look at a watch—it was eight o'clock.

A young Indian named Tito came forward. He, like the others, was a Tarahumara, and there was intelligence and pride in his demeanor. He obviously was a leader. Tito spoke to one of the geologists in Spanish, then issued instructions to the other Indians in Tarahumara. The language is harsh and guttural, and Tito added emphasis by shaking his head.

As a baby Tito had been abandoned by his parents because they were starving—a not unusual means to survival among the Tarahumara. He was found by a Mexican mule skinner who reared him as one of his family. The Indians never lost track of him, however, and he learned both Spanish and Tarahumara customs and language. This wilderness canyon was his home and these were his people, little touched by the civilization only a few hours away by rail.

Mexicans call his home Barranca de Cobre (Copper Canyon) and, since they first explored it in the 1690's, they have recognized it as one of the great mineralized areas of the world. The powerful attraction of gold, silver, copper, lead, and zinc have brought first the Spanish, then the Mexicans, to this wild, rugged area. With them came disease and slavery; the fear and distrust of the Tarahumara has its roots in the greed of their exploiters.

That afternoon, as the cliff shadows lengthened and the heat began to dissipate, the miners returned to camp, washed off the dirt of the day's labor by splashing in the cool river, and carried up to the campsite four large jugs that had been cooling in the stream. Tin cups were passed around and filled with *tesqüino*—a corn beer. Thus began a ritual, repeated daily in the mining camp. The geologists, offered a cup, accept it as a token of respect and friendship. In turn, the geologists pass out cigarettes and each Indian takes one and lights it, completing the friendship cycle. The beer flows freely and the Indians begin their story-telling, punctuating their language with much hand and arm motion, since story-telling to them is more than mere conversation.

An hour before sunset, darkness already was falling in the valley. The cooking fire, once again tended, provided a circle of light. Suddenly, without sound, another Indian stood at the edge of the flickering circle, waiting to be invited to join the group. The geologists were startled, but no surprise showed on the faces of the Indian miners. It was obvious they had heard the man coming for some time. In his arms the visitor held a small boy, clad only in torn and baggy trousers. The man spoke rapidly and with great emphasis to the miners. Tito, instantly at the man's side, spoke rapidly to the geologist in Spanish: "boy is hurt . . . fell off cliff and cut head . . . blood will not stop . . . need white man. Will white man help?"

Without a word one geologist spread his coat before the fire and ran to get a medicine kit and blankets while the other motioned for the father to come near the fire and lay the boy on the coat. The father hesitated, as the boy was bleeding badly, but the geologist took the youth gently and placed him on the coat. The boy, having lost a lot of blood from the deep cut, was in a state of shock and already cool to the touch.

Every mining geologist has to know more than just basic first aid, as accidents are frequent in mining. He must be prepared to tend broken bones, fevers, and the normal range of infections.

Both geologists worked quickly and efficiently. In a few minutes the bleeding was stopped, the wound sewed up, and the boy wrapped in blankets near the fire. Warm rocks were placed at his feet, color began to return to his face, and soon he was able to drink some coffee. The geologist produced some silver coins and Tito sent one of the miners off to the nearest hut to buy a chicken.

All through this process the Indians were quiet, watching every movement of the white men. Not missing the concern for the life of one of them, they noted that the white man used his silver to buy food for the boy, that he had used his own coat and blanket—and the boy's father did not even work for the white man! Such points were discussed in many ways as the beer drinking began again. These strange white men— so confusing!

Three days went by, and the boy grew stronger. Each meal he had meat, a luxury for the Indian. The geologist told Tito that by the next day the boy would be ready to go home. When Tito informed the boy's father, he was silent—an indication of respect for the white man's decision. Tito knew the father was concerned, because the white man had done him a favor. How could he repay it, when the white man owned everything? It was a difficult problem for the father, whose code did not permit him to take without giving. But what had he to give? The man sat quietly by the fire until long after the miners had gone to sleep. Then, without a sound, he crawled under his son's blanket to add his body warmth to that of the blanket and the fire.

The next morning the father took Tito aside and told him he must pay his debt to the white man but, since he was very poor, all he had to give was his labor. He would take his son and return to work for the white man without pay for as long as Tito thought proper. Tito turned away and looked into the morning mist that still hung in patches over the river. He was silent for a long time, but the father waited because Tito, understanding these strange white men, would know if his offer was proper.

Finally Tito turned back to face him and said, "You offer what is good and fair, but it cannot help the white men, since they must leave. They search for the bright shining rock, and they have not found enough of it. In two days we will all have no work. It is sad for all of us." The father, saying nothing, turned and went to wake his son. After breakfast he and the boy silently disappeared into the brush.

Early that evening the father appeared again at the edge of the firelight and awaited an invitation to join the group. Tito invited him, but his offer of food was politely declined. The father sat rigidly near the fire. All the Indians watched him as they hurriedly finished their meal. They sensed that something important was about to happen. When the first Indian had finished eating, Tito sent them to the river to bring jugs of *tesgüino*. Coffee was tossed out of the tin cups and the beer was poured. A cup was offered the visitor, but he declined with a shake of his head and reached into his rolled blanket to bring out a drinking gourd. Beer was poured into the gourd, and he joined in the drinking. When the geologist passed out cigarettes, he took one and smoked it.

Tonight there was no story telling, no chatter among the Indians. Even the geologists sensed an omen. Hours went by and the beer drinking continued. Tito had placed himself near the father, who had become the center of attention. Suddenly a torrent of words from the father shattered the silence. While he spoke words the white man could not understand, he looked at each of them directly.

Suddenly there was quiet and the geologist asked Tito, "What in the hell is all that?" Tito stood and faced the two white men, translating with great dignity. The faces of the other Indians gave no hint that they had understood what the father had said. They awaited the reaction of the white men. There was a debt of honor that must be repaid properly; who can say what these strange men would consider proper.

Tito knew he was the center of attention, and his Spanish words were slow and carefully spoken, without emotion or emphasis: "He says that he owes you for saving the life of his son, but he is a poor man and you are very, very rich and own the world, so he cannot give you what you do not have except to work for you for no silver coin, but you no have work to do, so he say he cannot repay his debt." Tito paused for breath, then he continued, "I know the white man look for the bright shining rock and I know where there is much such rock and I will show the white man and then I can repay my debt to him."

At this point Tito sat down and the eyes of the Indians carefully searched the faces of the white men. One geologist leaped to his feet. "Where does he say it is, Tito?" he asked. Tito put the question to the father, who walked with great dignity to the edge of the firelight and pointed across the valley to the huge mountain on the other side. He uttered a few words, raised his hands to indicate a length, walked back to the fire and rolled up in his blanket and went to sleep.

Tito translated: "It is there on the side of the mountain. Covered up, but it has this much bright shining rock in it [his hands were placed about one foot apart] and I will take you there with the light."

The geologists talked with each other, the Indians studying their faces intently. One felt it was a waste of time since the geology of that mountain was not right for silver and he had looked it over several times. The other wanted to see what the Indian had to offer. Tito was asked his opinion, but all he would venture was that there were many old Spanish mines and some Indians had found them, but they would not tell the white man for fear it would bring the Mexicans. These mine entrances remained carefully hidden.

Next morning the father, Tito, the geologists, and three miners set out to explore the side of the huge mountain. Hours passed, and everyone except the father became discouraged. The day was hot and there was little shade. Soon all the water was gone. The geologists would have liked to give up, but the father would not. About two o'clock he let out a yell and all rushed to his side. But what he indicated appeared to be no more than a snake or gopher hole.

The father spoke excitedly to Tito, who translated to the geologists: Here was the hidden mine, closed since the Indians had driven out the Spaniards (in the 1700's), but during World War II he and some other Indians had gone in and found the bright, shiny metal. They had taken a quantity of ore by pack mule to the smelter more than 350 miles away. When the Mexicans saw the rich ore, they tried to find the mine; but the Indians closed it again and it had not been touched since.

The geologists had the miners dig out the entrance and, in-

deed, there was an old mine. It was partially filled with mud
and rotted timber, but it definitely was an old Spanish mine.
Would it be worthwhile to clear it out? They would have to
check with those who were financing the venture.

A report was duly made to the investors at a meeting in
Chihuahua but, while one of the geologists believed an attempt should be made to explore the find, the other remained
skeptical. The Mexican investor declined to put up any more
money, since the rich vein the project had started out to explore had pinched out.

Still, the two *norteamericanos* who had invested in the project initially believed the old mine worth checking out. While
the investors themselves returned to the United States, the
geologists returned to the mine, distant a day's train ride and
another day by muleback.

Two weeks were spent in moving the equipment and campsite across the river and up onto the side of the mountain.
While this was being done, largely by hand because of the difficult terrain, other Indian miners were mucking out the old
mine. It was slow going, since rotted timber, small rocks, and
mud had gradually built up in the shaft, but there was progress each day.

On the third day a broken pick of the type used in Spanish
mines was found. The sixth day more old hand tools were uncovered. Suddenly the mine branched out into drifts leading
from the main shaft. It was a bigger mine than the geologists
had expected, but they feared it may have been worked out.
(Later the geologist would compute that it probably had
taken the Spaniards forty years with the tools of that period
to mine such an extensive area.) On the fourteenth day a
number of skeletons was uncovered and, just below them, the
bottom of the mine. It appeared someone had discovered the
mine but had not lived to work it.

The Indians climbed out to tell the gringo geologist that

they had reached the bottom. With his hand torch the geologist crawled in and then down into the mine. Each step on the ladder was slippery and dangerous, and the dank smell of the rotting wood and stagnant water was almost stifling. Finally he reached the bottom and shined his light in all directions but saw nothing of value. Searching the bottom carefully, he still found nothing. Then, searching the wall straight ahead, he found it caked with mud. He picked away at the face of it, and suddenly metal gleamed. Before him was a vein of rich silver and zinc ore eleven inches wide. The Indian father had remembered correctly. It would not even take an assay to show that this was rich ore. It was without question a major silver discovery.

Those who read this foreword to *El Lobo* may be surprised to learn that it is not a fictitious account, but an actual event that happened during 1970-1971. One of the geologists on site during the event was Bill Belk, who has assisted me in telling the story. The investor who made the decision in Chihuahua to reopen the old Spanish mine was myself.

If the story of El Lobo's life seems almost a tale of fiction, remember, when the locale is Mexico and the motivation is gold, silver, or power, truth will be even stranger than fiction.

                                        Aris A. (Bob) Mallas

Contents

EL LOBO
AND
SPANISH
GOLD

Prologue

EL LOBO STOPPED SUDDENLY on the trail ahead, took off his hat and bowed, and spoke a few words in the Yaqui tongue. It looked rather odd, for it was plain to see there was no one there for him to be greeting thusly. I thought for a moment he'd fallen victim to sunstroke. But then I heard the dreadful sound of a diamondback vibrating his *cascabeles* in unmistakable warning.

The Yaqui words seemed to soothe the reptile. El Lobo used a long stick to remove him from the trail, gently guiding, rather than pushing, the snake to a place of refuge under a giant cactus, to leave me room to pass. It was a curious procedure.

"El Lobo," I said, "I have observed that you never kill a rattlesnake. *¿Por qué, amigo?* Why is this so?"

"*Compañero,*" he replied, "as you know, I lived long with the Yaquis, and was married to the daughter of the old chief of the Bronco Yaquis, the brave, wild ones that the Mexican government tried so hard to exterminate; but who, instead, fought their armies to a standstill in the mountains and deserts of Sonora. The Yaquis have a rattlesnake god who lives

in a cave, high in the roughest mountains. They believe that
once a year all rattlesnakes in the desert report to this old
grandfather of all rattlesnakes. If you have been respectful to,
and have protected, rattlesnakes, this is reported to the rattlesnake god; you will prosper and no rattlesnake will strike you
intentionally. But if you accidentally step on one or walk too
close and he should strike you, you will not die, but only become sick so that you will be more observant in the future. If,
however, you kill one, the rattlesnake god will send out word
that you must be killed by the first rattler that can find op-
portunity to do so.[1]

"My Yaqui wife, Puñalita, and her people taught me the
proper words of respect, and that I must not harm any rattlesnake. I have never been struck, so it does no harm to respect
their beliefs. Whenever I address them with the Yaqui prayer,
I think of my lost Puñalita and my many friends among her
people. I also think of the rich gold mines that I once had and
worked in their country, and the good times and great adventures we had during those years."

He went on, telling me of many of the rich prospects he
and his Yaqui relatives—some of the best prospectors in all of
Mexico—had found and worked. As usual, he held my rapt
attention.

Of course El Lobo was not his real name. He was known by
many names in many places. I have called him El Lobo, for
in some of the mountains he was so known and at times the
name was pretty well deserved. I had known him in many

---

[1] The Yaquis, a Cahitan-speaking Sonoran tribe that aboriginally
occupied the flood-plain areas from the town of Sinaloa north to the
pueblo of Cumuripa, on the Yaqui River in Sonora, have a wealth of
myths and legends. Ruth Warner Giddings (*Yaqui Myths and Legends*)
tells the story of "The Snake People," in which a snake takes human
form to reproach a Yaqui boy who has attacked it with a stick but failed
to kill it.

places and in wildly different circumstances. I knew him when he was dead broke and appreciative of a few tortillas and a cup of chocolate offered by some peon with little else to his name, and when he was squandering a fortune. I knew him in the *campo*, in primitive mountain pueblos, in ancient, dangerous Spanish mines, and in semijungle *jacales*—and finally in the great *cárcel* in Toluca, where he had been sentenced to "thirty Aprils" on a homicide charge. He told me that he was innocent, and I believed him, as did many others who knew him.

Sure, he had been in fire fights and probably had killed, but these were standup shooting scrapes. He had many enemies in high places, and putting him in jail was a convenient way to get him out of their hair.

Admittedly, there's much about him I do not know. How could anyone know all there is about El Lobo? His real name was Richard Thompson, and to some he was known as Don Ricardo. He was the only son of a wealthy Southwest Texas ranching family, who had extensive financial interests otherwise. Partly responsible for his upbringing was an uncle who held large mining and railroad properties, and with whom young Richard spent much time in California and other Western mining areas. A precocious youngster, he learned much about mining, milling, and railroading. But discipline he never learned to abide. Indulged by others, he learned early to indulge himself, and therefore developed into the wild, swashbuckling character that he was.

In his teens he built his own plane, powered by a Harley-Davidson motorcycle engine, and flew it on his family's ranch. He soon was flying under power lines and bridges, the kind of stunting attempted only by the extremely confident, or the suicidal.

He considered schools a bore. Consequently, he managed to get thrown out of a number of good ones. Yet he was not completely uneducated. His spelling and grammar were strictly his own, but the same could be said of a lot of scientists with Ph.D.'s, whose competent secretaries deserve more credit than they get.

Intelligent and highly personable, El Lobo was dangerous and unpredictable when drinking. He stood more than six feet tall, was well muscled, and had great strength and stamina. Whether armed or not, he was not to be crossed.

Part of what I know of him I learned from various Mexican generals with whom he was associated, often in revolutionary activity. One of them looked upon him as a son, and many Mexicans who knew them both actually believed El Lobo was the general's illegitimate offspring.

I heard his name mentioned, too, in many out-of-the-way places in Mexico. He hadn't missed many of them, and in quite a few he left behind a blond child. He was obsessed with prop planes, steam railroading, prospecting, drinking liquor of any variety—*aguardiente*, mescal, rum, and Scotch or bourbon whiskey—and women, in that order. Drunk or sober, he could talk lucidly of his experiences and misadventures, but was always reticent about naming those whom he felt might be hurt.

In many ways, he was a gentleman born, in others an out-and-out buccaneer not above conning a sucker out of a sizable grubstake. He squandered several fortunes, one that he inherited and at least a couple he had made the hard way.

In his time, El Lobo was many things. He was a pioneer in modern aviation, and had owned and operated rich gold mines in northwestern Mexico. He and I were associated at one time in mining and other ventures. He was ever wild and unpredictable, but a good and loyal friend. He became a Lee Christmas[2] type of "Typical Tropical Tramp," but with a modern twist.

[2] Lee Christmas was a U.S. citizen who, between World Wars, involved himself in Guatemalan revolution and won a considerable de-

Though a competent locomotive engineer, he fought his revolutions in civilian airplanes, converted for military use. He involved himself in the shooting politics of many small, and some not so small, Latin American countries. In these small wars, his loyalties were predicated either upon pay or personal friendship. Not an idealist, he cared nothing for the voluble protestations of high purpose of those for whom he flew.

Some of the adventures of this fabulous character I witnessed personally. I learned of others during our evenings together in mining and prospecting camps, or in little Mexican hotels of isolated mountain pueblos. Some were unfolded in Mexican jails, where one is safe from his enemies and is able to rest and think and talk to old friends when they come to visit with him—and where he may have with him his wife or *dulce corazón*.

These adventures of El Lobo may seem implausible in the twentieth century, but I shared enough experiences with him to know they not only could happen but did. Almost any story having to do with mines or lost treasure in Mexico is colored by the fertile imagination of a superstitious people and, therefore, deserves a place in the folklore of that people. But it is not *just* folklore. That El Lobo's stories ring true to the Mexico he lived in is borne out by my own experiences.

The years that he spent prospecting and mining gold in northwestern Mexico, in the desert state of Sonora, were, I am sure, the happiest he had known, and he lived them to the full. He had great zest for life and I often felt that he regretted, far more than he admitted, having thrown all this away to become involved again in intrigue, revolution, and, eventually, exile.

---

gree of notoriety by seizing a number of towns and virtually controlling the country. He died in La Ceiba, Honduras, about 1940.

The story of his years in Sonora did not come to me in any chronological order. Some chance remark, a song, or a few Yaqui words spoken in a place far from the Yaqui homeland would start him reminiscing. He was a marvelous teller of tales around the campfire, with a prodigious memory for details of events long past.

He wanted his experiences written, and he thought I was the one to do it; so I stored these tales in my own memory until I had time to set them down. Perhaps they will help others to know the old *gambusino* as I have known him. El Lobo was no hero. He was not even always a good citizen. But he was my friend.

I don't know if you are still alive, Ricardo, still raising your own particular kind of hell—whether you are rotting in some dank cell of a Latin American jail, or have stood before a firing squad. But you wanted your story told, and I've tried to tell it in your own words. ¡*Salud*!

PART ONE

Yaqui Gold
and
Spanish Ghosts

1

The Teodorina Mine

OF ALL THE MINES I HAVE OWNED, the best producer was
the rich old Spanish mine that my Yaqui father-in-law,
Pluma Negra, took me to. It had been hidden by his people
almost two hundred years previously. There was absolutely
no sign that a mine had ever been there in that vast reach of
Sonora desert, so carefully and completely had the Yaquis
plugged the shaft and removed all traces of collar and dump.
They had smoothed the land and even transplanted desert
brush. The winds and drifting sand had completely obliterat-
ed all traces of any work of man. But even after two centuries,
the old man, having retained the story he had heard as a
child, unerringly led me to the location.

I had heard stories of the mine, the ghost of its first owner, and its fabulous richness since I had first started prospecting in the Altar district of Sonora. It was because of such stories that I had spent so much time in the area, where I eventually met my Yaqui wife, Puñalita, and all her wild relatives.

Hardly believing my good fortune at being taken so completely into the confidence of my Yaqui in-laws, I asked the old man if he would not take me to the mine, so we might open it up and make all of us wealthy. He went into the desert with me and traced the vein, panning good values right on the surface for nearly half a mile on each side of the vein's course. We were dry panning and blowing the waste away from the gold, and not being able to save much of the fine metal. When I asked the old chief where the shaft had been, he glanced about for bearings and walked a short distance from where we stood. Scratching the sand with a moccasined toe, he said, "*Aqui es el poso.* [Here is the shaft.]"

I thought Pluma Negra was playing a wry Yaqui joke on me, for I could not imagine any smart old Spanish miner digging in the empty desert with no more indication of mineralization than could be seen. The old chief pointed to the ground at his feet and told me to have the men start digging. Just below the desert sand we encountered rubble fill, and soon cleared the area of the old shaft that had been sunk by a Spanish grandee. We eventually cleaned from the shaft the rock with which it had been filled, finding many skeletons. This became the richest of all the properties I had and was the source of most of the gold that went through my mill at La Ciénaga, out from Caborca. After it was cleaned out and opened up so it could be worked, and I was finally able to persuade my superstitious miners to work in it, I produced hundreds of thousands of dollars in gold. This was the mine of the old Spanish ghost, Don Teodoro Salazar, who comes to La Ciénaga on windy nights—nights such as the one, so long ago, when he and all the Spaniards in La Ciénaga and throughout the district lost their lives in the fierce Yaqui uprising.

After I had married my Puñalita, we prospected and explored in many places: in the Sierra Madre, up the Río Fuerte in Sinaloa, and in the Altar district, as well as other localities in Sonora. We eventually went to La Ciénaga, which is, of course, the Spanish name for a swamp, but this place is really much more like an oasis. There is a little lake in the center of the pueblo, with date palms around it. It is isolated in the vast, dry, rough desert. There is some very rich dry placer around here and some good hard-rock prospects as well—more than I ever really got around to looking at, to say nothing of really prospecting and sampling.

When I decided to make La Ciénaga my home and headquarters, I bought a full block that had been Don Teodoro's hacienda. I got it very cheap as the heirs wanted to move south to a bigger and better town. La Ciénaga was only a dying mining town—almost a ghost town, with many empty homes and stores and only a few die-hard *gambusinos* [prospectors] and dry placer miners living there. There was one *tienda* [store] and cantina left, where the few miners, ranchers, and irrigated-cotton farmers traded. It had once been prosperous, giving employment to many men, but none of the mines had ever been reopened after the great revolution that started in 1910. Foreign capitalists do not take kindly to having their men killed and their properties destroyed.

We cleaned the place up and planted trees and flowers in the big gardens and patios, using lots of paint and whitewash to make the old, rundown building look respectable. The only trouble was that it was said to be haunted—full of ghosts, according to Pluma Negra and all of Puñalita's relatives. The Yaquis liked me, however, and did many things for me; so if the big, loco gringo that had married into their clan wished to live in a haunted house and mine the gold from haunted mines, that was fine with them. They said they would stick it out if I could, and they did. I have never believed much in spirits and ghosts, so I didn't care if they lived in the big house with us, as long as they didn't bother me or get in my way. There was plenty of room for a hundred people and any number of ghosts to live in the rambling old place.

It was a veritable fort, as were all of the big old Spanish homes and haciendas, built of stone and adobe, with big thick doors and shutters on the few windows that opened to the outside, and with rifle ports that would allow those within to resist almost any attack except artillery. The walls were thick, the flat roofs covered with several feet of earth. This is fine natural insulation and the rooms were cool in the hot desert. It was the finest house in the pueblo.

La Ciénaga is very old and is undermined by old mine workings and hidden tunnels that once connected the church with other parts of the town. This church was built during the early days of the Spaniards and is now in complete ruin, although not as old as the haunted one at the site of the old town of Caborca. At the edge of the little town there is a big, black slag dump and the ruins of the old Spanish smelter.

When I bought this property, only about twenty people lived in La Ciénaga. Like so many others in once-prosperous mining districts, it was almost dead. Many of the mines thereabouts had been worked even before Spanish times, for the Yaquis have been gold miners for as long as their history, handed down through thousands of years from father to son.

Mina Teodorina was not far from my *casa grande*. Both had once been owned by Don Teodoro Salazar. The ore was just rotten quartz held together with a lot of free, metallic gold. I had all this only because of Puñalita, my Yaqui wife. She was the daughter of one of the old Pluma Blanca's sons. Pluma Blanca had been one of the principal chiefs of the Yaqui nation during their wars with the Mexican government.[3] He was something of a military genius, and with his wild, fierce Yaquis, had defeated the Mexican armies several times and had been greatly feared and respected. Being the husband of old Pluma Blanca's granddaughter gave me prestige among the Yaquis of the Sonora desert and was a big advantage when prospecting and mining in their country, for it is still pretty much under their control. Many good prospects were shown to me by my Yaqui relatives and friends.

The story of the ghost of the old Spanish mine owner is an interesting one. Don Teodoro Salazar had come from Spain in a sailing ship nearly two hundred years before, landing at Puerto Libertad and prospecting inland. Eventually he found the rich outcrop in the desert, near the only water for miles in any direction. He worked this mine, called La Teodorina, for many years, taking tons of gold.

My father-in-law told me that Don Teodoro had enslaved many Yaquis, of whom large numbers were worked to death or died from the abuse of his heartless overseers. They mined the rich ore for the Spaniard. When their production did not come up to his demands, he would have a few of his Indian miners thrown into a big fire at the end of the week. This boosted the following week's production considerably.

At last the Yaquis got tired of it and revolted. They killed the Spaniard and his family and all the other Spanish people in the district. A few who escaped carried the news to the Spanish settlements to the south, but for many years no effort was made to subdue the Yaquis again.[4] The bodies of Don

[3] In 1825, after the Yaquis had been at peace with the government of New Spain for eighty-four years, they joined with Opatas, Lower Pimas, and Mayos to drive most of the Mexicans from the territory. Fighting continued, with occasional peaceful interludes, into the early part of the twentieth century.

[4] Jesuit missionaries, first sent to the Yaquis in 1617, lived peacefully

Teodoro and many of his people were thrown into his mine, and the waste dump was used to fill the shaft so that no one might know the location of the gold that had caused their enslavement and suffering. All evidence that a mine had existed was removed. It is difficult to conceive of a lot of wild Indians doing this with their bare hands, but they had done it. When I first saw the site, I could not believe that this raw desert concealed the wealth that I eventually took from it.

After the old Yaqui had shown me the location of the mine and we had reopened it, I found some sheets of gold as much as eight to ten inches across, as long as twelve inches, and from an eighth to a quarter of an inch thick, besides large nuggets and wire gold. There was lots of fine gold as well, and even the wall rock adjacent to the vein carried good values. This mine was, and still is, fabulously rich. The story of the mine, lost for so many years, had been handed down in the tribe for generations. My father-in-law was one of the few Yaquis who still knew its exact location and its history, and therefore was able to take me directly to it. Only because I was a member of the family did he do this, for no other white man had been able to find it and live very long afterward.

Years after the Spanish had been driven from all of Mexico, the railroad was built south from Nogales. An Englishman, or perhaps a German—my Yaquis knew only that he was not *norteamericano*, Spanish, or French—discovered float near the vein. Like all the dry placer and float that had weathered from the large vein, it was quite rich. Trenching revealed the outcrop, just below the shifting sand. It was either the main

---

with them until the 1740 revolt. A silver discovery in the Altar valley above Caborca led to a mining rush in the 1730's, and forced Indian labor customarily was used in the mines. The story told here gives rise to the supposition that Yaquis were brought from their homeland farther south to work in the Sonora mines, in Upper Pima country. These Yaqui slaves may have participated in the Pima revolt in 1751.

vein the old Spaniard had worked or another in the same system, for we found that rich veins of the system do outcrop in many places. Once we traced these outcropping veins for miles. It was of course impossible for the Yaquis to conceal all indications of rich ore in the desert as they had the old mine. In this later attempt to exploit the rich ore of La Teodorina, a shaft was sunk about two hundred feet west of the big vein, in country rock.

Whether this foreigner had information about the old Spanish workings or only stumbled onto the mine by accident, he was said to have found old Don Teodoro Salazar's mine before he, too, was killed. He took out much gold, but the Yaquis got tired of his way of doing things, as they had of the old Spaniard's, and he is somewhere down there in the workings, exchanging mining lore with Don Teodoro's ghost. I have heard many conflicting stories about this man, so I am not certain just what happened to him. In cleaning out the old workings, we never found any skeletons that looked to be much less than a couple of hundred years old. He may have been able to make his escape during the time of the great revolution, when so many foreign mining men were killed or driven from Mexico. It was after I had fixed up the *casa grande* and we had resumed our prospecting that Pluma Negra told me he knew the exact location of La Mina Teodorina.

I knew that I would need more miners than my small crew of Yaqui in-laws, so we went to Caborca and hired a crew of Mexican miners to help clean out the shaft. I set up a windlass and built a good shaft collar so we could work safely. I had quite a time keeping a crew working, for as we went deeper into the shaft, the Mexican miners found a lot of gold, which they high-graded from us. It didn't take them long to get rich enough to make their dreams of wealth come true,

and they would take off across the desert for Caborca or the
railroad, afoot. Often they just left when they got all the gold
they wanted, or thought they could get away with—not even
waiting for their pay. We were about a month in getting the
shaft opened all the way to the bottom, more than two hundred feet from the surface.

In the drift leading from the bottom of the shaft to the vein
we found many human bones, and quite a few had been found
while removing the rubble from the deep shaft. How many
men had been killed and thrown into the mine during the
revolt and the plugging of the mine was impossible to deter-
mine, for the bodies had been badly hacked up by the Indians.
The drift had been blocked only a short distance by the rubble
dumped into the shaft, and we soon got to the bottom and
into the workings.

There were many tunnels and small stopes that had been
only partly worked out, and high-grade ore showed in every
face. Some of the abandoned workings had been backfilled
with waste rock, and the many old ladders made of notched
logs, still as they were left when the Yaquis had attacked those
many years before, were so rotten they could be crushed in
our fingers. Four faces that had visible gold in the quartz vein
sparkled in the light of our carbide miner's lamps. The main
vein was beautiful white quartz, with flakes and plates of gold
all through it. Every fissure was gold filled. It was the petti-
est, finest, freemilling gold ore that may be imagined. In
addition to the high-grade picture rock, both the quartz and
much of the wall rock carried good values in fine gold.

The air was cool and fresh in this old Spanish mine; there
was no dead air, even when we first got it opened up, an unusual occurrence even in modern one-shaft mines. I was sure
that there must be another opening somewhere to allow air
circulation through the workings, but none of the Yaquis
knew of any other; nor did we find one during our exploration.

Many old mines are dangerous to enter, for they may be lacking in oxygen or contain deadly gas. The old workings are quite extensive and I never did completely explore them, for we found so much high-grade ore that there was no need to look for more. We kept busy taking out the ore, milling it, and spending money. We lived high for a long time and bought anything we wanted and went wherever we wanted to go.

This was, and still is, a fabulous mine and some of my Yaqui relations still work it in a small way whenever they need money. Although the Mexicans and Yaquis claim that the mine is haunted by the ghosts of the old Spaniards, I never saw or heard anything to make me believe this to be true. Maybe only Indians and Mexicans can see or hear the ghosts, for it was like any good mine, so far as I could see—except that it was a whole lot richer than most.

As always, however, I threw all of this away when I went back to flying for my revolutionist friends.[5] I was out of the country too many years and too much had happened after leaving my good mines and Yaqui relatives in Sonora for me to go back.

[5] El Lobo was engaged in the Sonora mine operations during the 1930's. He also flew planes to General Saturnino Cedillo, governor of San Luis Potosí, for Cedillo's revolution, and later was involved in political uprisings in Central America.

2

Land of *Bacanora*

WHEN I FIRST CAME to live with the Bronco Yaquis, before we found the Teodorina Mine, I had prospected all over the Altar district of Sonora. The hills called the Sierra Vieja have many good gold prospects. This is free gold, easily mined and milled with simple equipment. There also is much rich placer in and around these hills. It is dry placer, of course, and must be recovered with dry blowers or trucked to water to recover the gold, but it is rich and easily recovered. The Sierra Vieja is about twenty miles west of Caborca.

There is another range about twenty miles east of Caborca. From Caborca to these low mountains is a winding road, which I made out of a centuries-old pack trail many years ago so that my ore trucks could carry the ore from our mountain mines to my mill at La Ciénaga.[6] It was in La Ciénaga that I had my 35-ton Straub rib cone ball mill, powered with an old-time Hesselman oil engine. I had no classifier in the circuit, just a screen discharge to amalgamated copper plates about 3 feet wide and 16 feet long. From the plates, the tailings went to a Wilfley table, then to 6 wooden cyanide tanks, 12 feet high and 25 feet in diameter. I just leached the tailings without agitation and recirculated the solutions, then precipitated the gold in zinc boxes. The old 40-horsepower engine also drove a 110-volt direct-current generator that furnished lights and power for the pumps to transfer the leaching solutions.

I had a good man, a gringo cyanider, to run this plant. All I did was take care of the engine and run my mines and raise hell with my Yaqui relatives when we went to town for a good time. I had bought the mill just as it was and had only to make minor repairs to put it into operation, although it had been idle for several years. It had been operated as a custom mill for a long time by an old gringo who had died of old age and mescal, and I got it from his heirs. I made real money with this little mill and my good, high-grade, freemilling ore. I never used to go up to Arizona for a good time without my pockets full of thousand-dollar bills and plenty of raw gold. I have no idea just how many tons of ore I milled altogether, hell, I never kept count—just recovered the gold, spent money like water, and raised hell in Sonora and several places in the states.

I also had a leaching plant at Quitovac, a little desert pueblo south of Sonóita, with good cement and rock tanks. About

---

[6] La Ciénaga is not found on present-day maps. Nicolás de Lafora, with the Marqués de Rubí on his inspection tour of 1767, noted a La Ciénaga six leagues (about sixteen miles) from Aribaca Pass, as he proceeded along the Altar River toward Altar and Caborca, some sixty-five miles from old Caborca. The location referred to here, however, is forty to forty-five miles south-southeast of present Caborca.

fifteen miles from this plant there is a lone mountain where I found a deep inclined shaft. We built some small adobe houses and dug a good well and built two large *arrastres*, and I also had a Huntington mill there. We called our little settlement Costa Rica Nueva, and it is still shown on aircraft charts. There is lots of gold around there and we had lots of fun at Costa Rica. About ten miles south there is a trail leading west into a range of hills that parallel the road. At the end of this road are Las Hornitas and La Luz mines. I once owned them both.

Mina La Luz is in a big sill that covers about sixty acres and is about six feet thick. I took out tons of picture rock from La Luz, just high-grading. We would find a few specks of gold on the surface and start digging. Just a few feet down we would hit clean, white quartz, full of wire and leaf gold. The quartz would be all shot through with fine gold, as well. I would sometimes break off most of the quartz gangue and fill fruit jars with it, saving it until my next trip to Tucson, when I would take my good-looking Yaqui wife out on the town. We would go to the old Congress Bar and, after a few drinks, I would throw a jar full of gold up in the air. Puñalita would laugh to see the gringos in their good clothes scrambling on the floor for it, and fighting over what they found. I bought many small ranchos for my men and spent more money just having a good time than either of us is likely to see again.

About 45 miles farther south is Tajitos, once a large gold camp, but almost forgotten since the revolution. There is dry placer all around this place. West of Tajitos is La Mina Juárez. There are many good gold prospects in this range of mountains and, since the revolution, little work or exploration has been done. It is dry desert country and sometimes there is no rain for three years. Temperatures range from 125 to 130 degrees in the summer, but dry desert heat doesn't hurt when you are acclimated. This part of Sonora has a healthy climate and is fine desert country.

Between Yuma, Arizona, and Caborca, Sonora, there are many large sand dunes, where nothing moves but the blowing sand. Nothing relieves this waste of deep, drifting sand, extending south from the Mexicali-Sonóita highway for about seventy miles, except the lone peak of an extinct volcano, Sierra Pinecate, about thirty miles from the border. It appears dark reddish to black from the air and sticks up out of the desert like the sharp peaks of the moon. For many miles around it are vast lava flows. The lava usually is deeply covered by the drifting sand, but sometimes the lava flow blows clean. This little mountain has two or more craters, one of them about a mile or more across. This large crater has grass and trees growing in it, and natural tanks where water collects when it rains. There may even be springs inside it. The Yaquis tell many strange stories of this mountain and the crater.

My Yaqui father-in-law, Pluma Negra, once told me of a fight he had led against troops of Pancho Villa that resulted in their annihilation on this mountain.[7] Villa's troops had lost a big battle at Álamos, far to the south. Part of his forces, having become separated from the main body, rode north after the battle. At Santa Ana the Yaquis jumped them. Most of the Villistas were killed, but about a hundred who were well mounted got away and headed northwest, into the desert. Whether they thought they could lose the Yaquis in the desert, then turn east toward Chihuahua, where they would be safe,

[7] The enmity of the Yaquis for Villa's troops likely stemmed from their support of Alvaro Obregón, who was Villa's enemy in the revolutionary decade, 1910–1920. Many Yaquis fought valliantly in Obregón's forces, on his promise that with victory he would restore their lost territory and liberty. When he ascended to the presidency of Mexico, however, the promises were quickly forgotten.

or that they could safely cross the desert will never be known. All Mexicans fear and respect the Yaquis, and these men of the great Pancho Villa may have been riding blindly in attempting to escape them. No man knows the desert like the Yaquis. The terrible heat reflected from the hot, white sands is normal and natural to them. The waterless desert is their natural environment. Yaquis can lie covered by the sand and rest or sleep without being seen at close range. They know where to find water and the safe routes to travel.

When the remnants of the Villistas started into the desert, they were as good as dead. The Yaquis just let the desert take care of them, with a little help from themselves. The troops were well armed, while the Yaquis had only bows and arrows, so they avoided any direct meeting. Pluma Negra and his people would show themselves occasionally and let their enemy taste a few Yaqui arrows, just to keep them moving deeper into the desert, away from the water holes. When the soldiers were far out in the sands, toward the drifting dunes surrounding the peak, the Yaquis came out in large numbers and let fly many arrows. As more of the Mexican troops lost their lives, the others fled on into the desert, finally to find refuge in the crater. Now they were better off than the Yaquis, for the crater had water, and probably game.

The chief called his most powerful witch doctor. It is always good to have a powerful witch doctor on your side. This one was very old and his medicine was strong. He sat down in the sand and opened the skin pouch in which he carried the tools of his trade. He laid out his frog and lizard skins, dried bugs, bits of bone, and other powerful medicine and went to work. After about an hour of making medicine, he called the chief and told him to get his men ready; the enemy soon would be coming out of the crater, fast. The old witch doctor then fell into a sort of trance and his body became rigid. The chief's men carried him and his medicine to a safe place in the rocks where he would not be hurt or killed in the fight they knew was coming, for his medicine had never failed them. Drawing close to the crater entrance, they hid in the wide cracks in the lava behind the many large boulders, spewed out of the volcano ages ago. While the soldiers had food and arms, they were now afoot. The Indians had killed or captured their horses and mules.

Suddenly the Mexicans came running from the crater, as though all the devils of hell were after them. Over them hung a dark cloud, and they were screaming and waving their hands. Running in all directions, they made no effort to defend themselves. They threw their guns away as they ran. Many fell down and rolled in the sand, then jumped up and ran again. The Yaquis just stood and stared at their antics, forgetting to shoot at their now-defenseless enemy. Then they began to kill with arrows at close range. The black cloud, which they now could see was an enormous swarm of bees, turned and flew back into the crater.

Pluma Negra told me that after all the Mexicans had been killed and the Yaquis had eaten well of the captured food and taken the guns and ammunition from the dead, they went into the crater to fill their water gourds. While he was there he looked for signs of gold. He was a good prospector. As a young boy, he had been captured and sold by the Mexicans and had been taught much of mineralogy and geology by a priest. While in the crater he found vesicular lava with amygdules of what appeared to be silica with gold. He kept several samples for many years, because he had never seen gold in such a rock. He was sure that there must be much gold in the crater, although he had found only boulders of float with golden amygdules, all of which came from a little arroyo leading from the crater into the desert. He told me that, if I liked this ore, we might be able to go to the crater and find a big deposit. Several days after telling the story, he brought a piece of the vesicular basalt with many gold-filled cavities. It was very rich ore, although I, too, had never heard of such an occurrence of gold. We decided to go to the crater and look for the mother lode—sometime, maybe. We had lots of good ore that kept our mill running and gave us about all the money we could spend, so there was no hurry about trying to get to the crater.

My father-in-law and all of his people believed that the old witch doctor's powers had caused the swarm of bees to attack the soldiers. Undoubtedly they had disturbed the swarm when they were getting water or making their camp in the crater, causing the bees to swarm around them and sting. No simple explanation such as this would have been acceptable, however, for their faith in the old witch doctor could not have been shaken.

The Yaquis, like many other Indians, do have certain powers for which our white minds can find no explanation. They are able to communicate with each other even though they may be many miles apart. Of this I am sure, for I have seen too many demonstrations of such ability to have doubts. Many times my Yaqui wife, Puñalita, would get news out of thin air; there had been no visitors and no possible normal way of communication. We had neither telephone nor telegraph at La Ciénaga, and there would not have been time for a rider or even someone traveling in a car or truck to have brought the news that she told me matter of factly, as though she couldn't understand that I, too, did not have this power.

I remember one instance in particular. She told me that two gringos had camped at a certain spring, nearly a hundred miles away. She said they had given some of her relatives some canned tomatoes, that one had a thirty-thirty rifle, nearly new, and the other an older carbine of the same caliber. Describing the two men, she said they would arrive at La Ciénaga that night. At first I thought some traveler had stopped by and told her all this, but there had been no car or truck—only a few local horsemen who could not have ridden so far in such a short time. It was always as she told me. This time the two men showed up just as she had said they would, and the descriptions of them and their weapons were uncannily accurate. How do they do this? Is it perhaps some kind of mental telepathy? Maybe it is the sort of thing that scientists are beginning to know as extrasensory perception, developed to an extremely high degree among this particular people. I do know that the Yaquis do not communicate by drum signals, or by fast runners, as do the Tarahumaras.

A short time after the old chief told me of the gold in the crater, I cashed in a lot of gold, exchanging it for United States currency at Hermosillo, for I wanted to take a good vacation in the states with my pretty Yaqui wife and buy a new plane. I told Puñalita to dress in her best Yaqui clothes—deerskin with plenty of gold and turquoise—and to wear her best Indian boots. The mountain Bronco Yaqui dress much like the Navajo, but wear more fine deerskin, like the Apache. They also buy cloth and make clothing from it, but the old dress is much better for hard service in the mountains and on the desert. I always asked my wife to dress as the daughter of a Yaqui chief should, but she also liked the junk they sell in stores. Many times she would put on a store-bought dress that I had paid fifty or a hundred dollars for in Tucson or Phoenix, then get on a wild horse and ride right out of the damn thing. She had long hair that fell to well below her waist. She wore it in a sort of horsetail, and in it she carried a long, sharp knife that she could throw like an arrow. That's why she was called Puñalita, or Little Dagger. She could kill a chicken with this knife from as far away as most men might throw a stone. She did her hair up in a lot of pure gold and silver rings, with a lot of oil or grease, as most Indian women do.

I wanted her to see how gringos live in their own country and also to show her off to some people I knew in the East. That's why I wanted her to wear her very best Indian clothes and ornaments. I also told her to carry a complete extra outfit with her, for we would travel far to the cold North of Los Estados Unidos del Norte. I said to her, "If you will dress real nice for me so that I may take you wherever I go with pride, I will buy you a box that sings in Spanish, and also in gringo—just like the big boxes that they have in some of the fine houses of the rich in Mexico City, which you saw and heard when we visited my friends there. This box will be very small, and you may carry it with you wherever you go and it will sing and make music for you. I will also buy you maybe ten dresses—the finest that we can find in the gringo stores."

"All right, my lord," she said (that is the way a Yaqui wife addresses her husband). "I will dress as you wish, my lord. You do not have to pay me to do this, but about this box that you speak of, so very small, that sings Spanish songs; this I will have to see to believe. When do we leave for *el norte*?"

"Tomorrow at daylight. Get your turquoise sorted out and have your sisters help you dress." She had a chain made of hundred-dollar gold pieces that had been drilled and strung on ordinary baling wire. The Yaquis have lots of both U.S. and Mexican gold coins hidden out. Much of this gold probably was taken from the railroad express cars destroyed during their long years of war with the Mexican government. They had robbed many trains on the Sud Pacífico de México. Only about twenty-five years before I came to live with the Yaqui, they were still robbing and burning trains. Once they had taken up miles of track and piled the ties in great heaps, burning them to heat the rails, which they then tied in knots.

We got a good early start next morning and at last arrived at the little pueblo of Santa Ana, on the railroad about eighty-five miles south of Nogales. We came out of the high mountains of the Sierra Madre, west of Santa Ana. The peaks were snow covered, for it was January. We boarded El Rápido in Santa Ana and soon were in Nogales. With the help of friends in Nogales, I was able to get a *permiso* for Puñalita to enter the United States by showing the Immigration Service officers our wedding certificate. We rode up to Tucson in a taxi and arrived just in time to board the eastbound passenger train. It was a good train, with Pullmans and club car, but we had not had time to get tickets. Our luggage was only my small leather bag, mostly full of money and nuggets, and my wife's Indian war bag of deerskin, in which she carried her extra clothes and jewelry. I had a lot of thousand dollar bills, five hundreds, and hundreds, all in U.S. banknotes—over a hundred thousand dollars altogether—and about fifteen or sixteen pounds of raw gold. We had just climbed aboard from the taxi, without reservations or tickets—nothing except what we had left the mine with that morning.

I led the way to the club car and as we made our way through the Pullmans, people turned and stared. I heard someone say, "They are from the movie outfit that is making a picture out here. I saw some other movie people aboard the train. She still has her makeup on; must have left in a hurry."

We finally got forward to the parlor car and sat down. I ordered Scotch and soda and soon the conductor came through. I told him to try to fix us up with a drawing room, or the best he had, and to get us tickets through to New York.

I gave him a thousand-dollar bill, and he said that he could get us a drawing room, and also the tickets, but that I would have to change trains at Chicago. "That's fine," I told him, "Just line us up with the tickets and keep the change." Pure struck-it-rich prospector style.

He looked at the thousand-dollar bill and shook his head and said that he couldn't keep the change and, if I had it, please give him something smaller. Just for fun, I opened the leather bag beside me and said, "Well, *capitán*, I'll see what I can find in here. Down south, where we come from, they don't have many small bills, but I'll sure look." The bartender rolled his eyes until they were nearly all white when he saw the packs of hundred, five-hundred, and thousand-dollar bills, with a lot of loose ones and all the loose gold that I had just thrown into the bag. I said to the conductor, "*Capitán*, I can give you some hundred or five-hundred-dollar bills, if they will do."

He got kind of shakey and said, "Man, you had better let me put this in the safe in the mail car; you can't carry that much money around loose on the train. Who knows what kind of people may be aboard? I don't want any robbery or murder on *my* train."

I snorted and said, loud enough for everyone to hear, "Hell, *capitán*, I've got my Yaqui wife with me, just let anyone start off with this bag and see how far he gets. She kills at twenty yards with that knife she carries."

He looked at her hard, then at me, and said, "Just who in hell are you people anyway?" I laughed and told Puñalita in Yaqui what he had said. She thought it a very big joke, and laughed hard.

He was all shaken up about us and the money and gold. "Work for the movies, huh?" he said. "That wife of yours sure does look like an Indian all right. What picture are you people making?"

I tried to explain, but it was all over his head. I guess that he figured the world ended at the Mexican border. He walked away shaking his head and muttering about crazy movie people.

I ordered more drinks and gave the bartender a nice big nugget and told him to have it made into a tie pin. He asked, "Is that really gold, sho nuff?" A lot of people came around to look at the raw gold as they always do when they find out you have some, and I bought drinks for everyone. We were all just one big happy family right quick. It sure is funny what a few drinks of Scotch and some nuggets will do to get everyone acquainted in a club car on a crack train.

By and by, the conductor came back with our tickets and said that he would wire ahead at the next stop for a drawing room for us from Chicago to New York. He wouldn't accept a tip, but he sure did like the big nugget I gave him. I told him, like any damn fool prospector going on the town with his pockets full of gold, "If I had just run my mine and mill another couple of months before taking this vacation, I could have avoided having to change trains. I would have just bought both railroads and hooked them together." Again he walked away shaking his head.

I wasn't too far off at that, for if some of my mines had been worked as they should have been, I probably could have bought controlling interest in both lines. The railroads weren't doing as well as I was in those days, for it was during the depression in the states—something we didn't know anything about in the land of the *bacanora*[8] and rich gold mines.

Puñalita spoke no English, and not a whole lot of Spanish, for the Bronco Yaquis of the mountain desert have never been smoothed out much by the Mexican government. Some Americans and their wives tried to talk to her, but she could only laugh and offer them her drink. Not understanding what they were saying, she couldn't answer their questions. She tried to talk to them in Yaqui and in her poor Spanish, but I think most of them thought she was making a big joke. She was very light for a Yaqui and very good looking. She had a sort of strong, solid look and, in her fine Indian clothes, looked rich and strong. I was very proud of her.

[8] A Yaqui liquor somewhat like a mixture of mescal and tiswin (an alcoholic drink made by the Apaches), said to taste like kerosene.

After several days on the train and a few little adventures, such as my wife sticking her long knife into the back bar from the other end of the car—just for fun—we arrived in New York City with our money and gold. It was a cold winter in the North, with little sun. We felt the cold keenly after having been so long in the sunny desert of Sonora, until we bought warm woolen clothes. I then went into a radio store and bought the best portable radio in the place. It played well and sang very nicely, too, I thought. I handed it to my wife and told her that this was the little box I had promised her, that it would play music for her wherever she might be. She gave me a dirty look, but took it and walked out. I asked her what was wrong.

"This box is not what you said you would buy for me!" she said. "It speaks only gringo. Not one word of Yaqui or Spanish has it said. And it plays only gringo music. You know that I do not speak gringo. Why did you not buy one as you said you would—one that speaks and sings in Spanish and plays good Mexican music?" She had no understanding of radio, and had heard one only a few times, as I had never bought one for my home at La Ciénaga.

"When we get back to Arizona—maybe before, if I can find the new plane I want—it will speak and sing very well in Spanish," I promised. But she was not satisfied.

"Who will teach it to sing in Spanish? You do not speak much Spanish and you cannot sing at all."

I laughed, for she, like most Indians who had never been around American cities, was childlike in many of her thought processes. This I did not mind, for she was sharp as a tack in everything that was important in the desert and mountains, where it really counted.

I said, "Hell, it will learn these things at once; that is the way it is made. It sings and speaks the language of whatever country it's in. Soon it will be singing and speaking the best Spanish and playing all the Mexican music that you like."

After spending a week and a lot of money and buying many things and going with her to see many wonders of this great city, I went to the airport where I had left word of the kind of ship I wanted. They had a good Pacemaker Bellanca without a lot of useless radio and blind flying equipment, the way I wanted it. This plane is good for heavy loads and short fields—a really fine ship, safe and strong.

I wired a general in Mexico City who was a very good friend, and who was in favor, and asked him to arrange for clearances for the plane. He wired back and said that he would take care of all clearance papers for entry at Brownsville, Texas, and that if I would send him the information needed for Mexican licensing he would have the license waiting for me at the border. After sending the information, we took off for Texas. All I cared about was clearance for the Mexican side. Some Mexican officials who were very narrow in the head did not like to give me clearance for airplanes at that time.[9]

The general fixed everything up fine for me and I cleared for entry with no difficulty. We flew to Monterrey, Nuevo León, to see my friend, General José López Zauzua, and other friends, then off for Sonora, the mines, and home. We stopped along the way to visit with some of my old friends, both pilots and miners, as well as a couple of old generals that I had flown for a time or two.

High over the sierras the sun shone brightly on our silver wings. Life was very good. Above La Ciénaga I throttled back

---

[9] El Lobo admitted to smuggling many kinds of military contraband, including airplanes, and his predilection for flying for revolutionary armies had not endeared him to the parties in power in several Latin American countries.

MANUEL

the engine and let down in big, long circles, just looking over the desert and my mine and mill and enjoying being alive. Down, down we came and landed in the main street. I owned most of the town and landed wherever I damn pleased. The dirt street was wide and long. It started in desert at one end and ended in desert at the other. Kids, burros, and dogs scattered in every direction as the Bellanca rolled down the street to my *casa grande.*

The box that talked and sang had learned to speak good Spanish by this time, and also made beautiful Mexican music, but so far it hadn't said a word in Yaqui. But Puñalita was happy, the day was beautiful, and we were again in Sonora. *Con el favor de Dios,* God's grace, we had made it safely home.

The world was a fine place in those days. ¡*Viva México*!

3

Wild Man of Caborca

WHILE I WAS LIVING at La Ciénaga and mining all around there, sometimes a few gringos would show up, usually lost and out of water. One in particular has stayed in my memory, for we had lots of fun together. This wild gringo, whom we had saved from dying out on the desert, stayed with me a long time. He and my Yaquis got along fine together.

He was a big man, about 6 feet 3 or 4 inches tall and weighing about 250 pounds. He was pure iron, no fat at all, and was a heavyweight prizefighter. He had sparred with many of the big names in boxing, and had won over a lot of good men in his time. He was about 35 years old when he came through the Sonora desert on El Rápido, the passenger train of the Sud

Pacífico de México. He had been traveling with a lot of people on their way to Guadalajara, Jalisco, then to Mexico, D.F., where the big gringo was to train some Mexican fighter they thought was a coming champ.

Out in the middle of the desert he had got drunk and fallen off the train. He was all bruised up, had a badly wrenched leg, and was nearly dead from thirst when we came along and found him, sprawled out unconscious beside the track. We carried him to La Ciénaga and gave him water and food. My Yaquis doctored his cuts and bruises, and in a couple of weeks he was as good as new. He liked Indian life, as we lived it, so well that he wanted to stay and help with our prospecting and mining.

The poor fellow was punchy but very strong. He was the biggest man my Yaquis had ever seen. His body was completely covered with long, black hair—like an ape. He let his beard grow long and, with his face burned black by the desert sun, he sure did look rough. We had a lot of ocelot and lion skins, so my Yaquis and I thought it would be interesting to make a wild-man outfit for him and have some fun with people who didn't know about him. He liked the idea and put on a convincing act in his wild-man clothes. He made horrible faces and roared and grunted and hopped around like a real wild man.

Sometimes on Saturdays we would go to some other small town and make the rounds of the bars with our "wild man." I would take two of my dump trucks, loading up all my wild Yaqui crew of miners, Puñalita and her whole family, and the wild man. We were a wild outfit and no joke about it. Everyone was armed to the teeth with knives, guns, and machetes. We had no opposition wherever we went. No *policía* ever showed up. They made for their holes whenever we came to town, for we had them outnumbered and outgunned. The businessmen and cantina owners didn't want to antagonize me or my crew for we were good pay and always left a lot of money in their tills whenever we paid them a visit.

My Yaquis didn't like Mexicans, however; especially vaqueros, for the vaqueros looked down on miners. Often there would be fights between them and sometimes someone would get badly cut up or shot, but we always took care of things and I tried to keep my wild gang in line as much as posssible. The big gringo thought this was the life for him. He was always willing to help the fun along.

One time we loaded him in a truck in his wild-man clothes and hung a chain on him and fastened it with a padlock. The chains were loose enough for him to get out of them when the time came. We went to Caborca, where no one had seen him yet, and stopped at the biggest bar. I bought drinks for everyone. My Yaqui father-in-law, Pluma Negra, told the fat *cantinero* that we had caught a wild man and had him chained up in the truck, and that we planned to sell him. We went out to the truck and brought the wild man in for everyone to see, and to buy him a drink. Three of my biggest Yaquis dragged him in by the chains while the wild man roared and snarled and struck at them with his manacled hands and feet. He made a hell of a noise and terrible faces while the Indians pretended to beat him with the loose ends of the chains. When he jumped toward the barman, screaming and trying to grab him, it was more than the poor man could stand. He flew out the door and ran all over town telling people that the wild man was getting loose—which he was, for he could get out of the chains whenever he wanted to, the way we had them fixed. We had a wild time for the rest of the night. Finally we got tired of the wild-man business and were ready to start for home.

On the way into town we had shot an eagle, hitting him in one wing, hurting him just enough to enable us to catch him. We had thrown him in one of the trucks and put some old

serapes over him, for I wanted to keep him alive. We had for-gotten all about the big bird, with all the fun and drinking of many bottles of tequila. The wild man and a couple of his Indian pals got into the truck with the eagle. They were all drunk as hoot owls—*tecolotes muy borrachos*—and none of them remembered the big eagle under the serapes. The night had turned cold, as it often does on the desert, and they picked up the serapes to cover themselves. That's when all hell broke loose. The eagle had recovered from shock and was in a real mean mood. He attacked the first thing that moved—our wild man. Sinking its long talons into the fighter's back, it started to chew him up with its sharp beak. That damned eagle put the finishing touches on making our wild man wild. The big fellow fell out of the dump truck and rolled on the ground, trying to get rid of the bird and screaming at the top of his voice. The two Indians who had been in the truck with him tried to get the eagle off his back, and they were getting cut up badly, too. They were all a bloody mess.

A lot of town Indians and Mexicans who had come to see the wild man really got an eyeful. They are probably still talking about it. He put up a real fight with the eagle's claws sunk into his tender back and doing its best to carve steaks out of him with its beak, and all the while beating hell out of him with those big, strong wings. The big bird sure didn't act wounded any more. The poor wild man jumped and turned flip-flops and rolled on the ground, screaming and begging us to get the damned thing off of him. His two Indian friends finally got the eagle loose. Puñalita and I were so stunned that all we could do was stand and stare. The whole thing had happened so fast that we didn't realize any more than the others, except the two who were fighting the eagle, what really was happening. If it hadn't been for these two, drunk as they were, our wild man would have been in a bad way. When they finally got the eagle off of the poor man, it tried to get at them but finally flew off into the night, as though it had never been hurt.

Another time, two gringos got lost in their light plane. They had been flying from New York to Los Angeles and had run into strong cross winds at about ten thousand feet and wound up out of gas, in the desert. We found them in pretty bad shape from the heat and dehydration. They had been two days without water on the desert, with no shade except from the wings of their ship. After giving them water, we took them to my little town of La Ciénaga. I fixed up a place for them to stay in my big house until they got their strength back and could fly again.

These men had always lived in big cities in the East and had never been in the West before. They had landed with a dead stick, deep in the wild Sonora desert, when they should have been in Yuma, Arizona. Both had heard a lot of wild stories about Yaquis, so they expected that just about anything could happen to them, including getting scalped. They were both wealthy; one was a banker, the other an automobile dealer. When they saw the rich gold ore that I was working, some fruit jars of placer gold, and some high-grade tungsten ore that I had, it set them wild.

You have seen what the sight of raw gold will do to some people. Otherwise normal, intelligent men will lose their heads when they get a little gold in their hands. I had a hard time convincing these two that I didn't want to sell out, sell an interest, or take any part of their money. After they got to feeling better, several days after I had found them, I decided to have some fun.

I told my Puñalita that these people were from New York, where rich people such as they did not drink plain water, but always drank half water and half alcohol. Remembering how cold it had been in New York while we were there, she could believe that some people might need some inner warmth to keep going in such a country. She decided that we must make them feel at home until they had completely recovered from their ordeal in the desert. We would make sure that they had everything according to the custom in their own homeland, for the gringos had been kind to us.

I said to her, "See to it that they get no water unless it is half alcohol, and tell your sisters and the servants."

She looked at me as though she didn't quite believe me, but a Yaqui wife never questions what her husband says. "Yes," she replied, "yes, my lord, I will do as you say, for we must treat them well. Poor men, they have suffered much from the heat and thirst and we must do all we can for them."

We had a big *olla* [porous clay water jar] that was always kept full of water and which hung in one of the rooms of the big rambling old house. Evaporation kept it cool and sweet in the big *casa*, for it was always cool, compared to the temperature outside.

We always had plenty of alcohol, for we sold it in our miner's bar and also used it in an alcohol stove. I always bought alcohol in fifty gallon drums, for it is cheap in Mexico. The big *olla* was filled with the high powered mixture of alcohol and water, as were all the other water jugs in the house. I told my *cantinero* to serve the two gringos no water unless it, too, was half alcohol. My Yaquis were only trying to please the gringos. They spoke no English and not much Spanish, and the two Americans could speak only English.

Our wild man was away at a new prospect with some of my Yaquis, so these two gringos hadn't seen him yet. They were completely helpless as far as being able to get even a single drink of pure water was concerned. The well was inside the house, and they didn't go into the *cocina* [kitchen]. They were lost in the big old place, which covered nearly a city block. They were more than half afraid of my long-haired, half wild and rough looking Yaqui outfit.

Still somewhat dehydrated from the desert heat, they wanted lots of water. They would start to drink a glass full, frown and say to me, "This water smells and tastes like alcohol. What is in it?"

"Just these damn minerals," I said. "Everything is loaded with gold and silver and copper and tungsten around here. That is what gives it an odd taste. You will soon get used to it." I had told them not to drink from the little *ciénaga* because it was loaded with diamond dust and would cut their guts out.

One of the gringos took a big swallow of the doctored-up water, smiled a big smile and said, "Mineral water, hell! Not bad, not bad! But it sure tastes like alcohol."

I said that it was not as good as the water higher up in the mountains, but was a lot better than no water, or the diamond water out in the *ciénaga*, anyhow. It might taste strange to anyone not used to it, but it was good water and everyone that lived here drank it without any ill effects. After a few drinks neither of them felt any pain. By noon they were both drunk as lords.

Next day they both begged for water, just plain water, even diamond water—guts or no guts. I heard one of them say to the other, "My God, what a hell of a country! And the damned water—I'd give a thousand dollars for just one drink of plain old New York water now. How in hell do these little kids here drink it? It's pure dynamite. What a place! These people are millionaires but they live in mud houses and sleep on the floor on grass mats. They have fine cars and new trucks and diesel engines and gold in every box and bag around the place, and everything that isn't gold or silver is copper or tungsten. They drive fine cars over the desert on sharp rocks and don't give a damn for tires, and they eat a fruit that grows on corn stalks that they call tamales. These tamales taste like meat or something that has been cooked, but you can see they just cut them off of the corn stalks and warm them and eat them."

Yaqui tamales rolled in a corn husk do look like an ear of corn, so perhaps they couldn't be blamed for believing that was the way we got them. These two poor fellows had been through quite a lot and had seen many things that were strange to them during the few days they had been at La Ciénaga. They were just about ready to believe anything. Finally, I took pity on them and gave orders that they should be served pure water again. When they asked about the change in taste, I told them it was the same as before; they were just getting accustomed to it.

Soon they felt so much better that I sent a truck with gas to carry them to their plane. They flew it to La Ciénaga and landed it on the little race track where we sometimes had horse races. They now wanted to see some of my mining operations. I told them that I would be glad to show my mines to them, but "right now it isn't very safe to go to the mountains where the mines are."

They asked why it should be any more dangerous than where they were. Guess they figured things were pretty dangerous right in our town. I said, "This is the time of year that the wild man comes down out of the high Sierra Madre. He really is a bad one, and we don't try to do much work when he is around. Last year he almost got my wife, and three of my Indians are still missing since he was here. Puñalita is very fast on her feet and he couldn't catch her, or she wouldn't be here right now!"

They didn't laugh when I told them this; they were conditioned to believe almost anything by now. They just wanted to know more about the wild man.

"Well," I said, "I really don't know much about him, and I'm not too anxious to learn. He never bothers us here at La Ciénaga, and we don't go into his territory. That way things work out very well for all concerned. Every year about this time he comes down out of the mountains and catches a few women to take back with him. Guess they don't last very long. He tears any man he catches apart, and even the wildest and toughest Yaquis are afraid of him."

I could see that they really were serious about wanting to get a look at the wild man. They asked all sorts of questions about him, so I told them as well as I could about his fierceness and his wild appearance. "Some kind of ape man," they decided, seriously. "We should trap him and take him to the States. A thing like that would really be something in New York!"

They had taken the bait, so I kept at them. "Why don't you try to trap him, then?" I suggested. "I will pay you well to take him to hell away from here. I'll give you chains and guns and anything else you need, just to get rid of him!"

They thought about it, and said, "We can't do it ourselves, but we can get some people who can catch him alive, people who have caught wild apes in Africa!"

I told them that the wild man would go back to his hideout in the Sierra Madre in another week or so, for he probably had caught all the Indian women he wanted by now, and we probably wouldn't see any more of him for another year. I told them that there were some Indians hereabouts who would like to shoot or capture him, for the wild man had caught some of their women. "They would be glad to go with you. Then you fellows could see what you could do about catching him. Here is a good thirty-thirty carbine. Shoot the s. o. b. if you get the chance!"

But they both said, "No, no! We don't want to kill him, we want him alive." I convinced them to take the rifle anyhow, for they might need it for protection in case the wild man jumped them; he wouldn't know the difference between Indians and New Yorkers. I also offered them some bear traps and suggested they bait them with chunks of beef; if they caught him, the Indians could tie him up before they took him out of the trap.

I sent a couple of my Indians ahead with a note to the wild man, telling him of my plan. He was to dress in his wild-man outfit, hide in one of the mine tunnels, and run out and raise some hell when the gringos showed up. Taking one thirty-thirty, I gave them another. I had loaded the one I gave them with cartridges from which I had removed the powder, except for a few grains. Thus, the bullet would just clear the barrel, but could travel no more than a few feet. I didn't want my wild man to get hurt in case one of these gringos stampeded and fired at him point blank.

I left the two men, with a couple of my Yaquis, off at one of the other older workings. I had coached the Indians to act scared and panic when they came upon the wild man. All the Indians thought the wild-man joke wonderful. They were a little afraid of him anyhow, he was so big and strong and fierce looking. They had all heard the legends of *los gigantes*, the giants whose bones are sometimes found on the desert, and who are thought by many to have at one time been fairly numerous and of fairly high intelligence. They probably thought our wild man was one of these big people they had heard of from their childhood story tellers.

My plan was now to have the wild man go into one of the tunnels of the mine where I had left the two gringos, then arrange to have them come underground with me. Here they would meet the wild man under the scariest conditions I could think up. I drove up to the new prospect where he was working, brought him back with me, and left him at one of the other entrances. The place was out of sight of the gringos,

who were standing on the dump before the portal of one of
the adits, going over the dump for free gold specimens, when
I returned.

We popped the flint on the carbide lamps and went into the
drift with the Indians. The gringos had found some good
specimens on the dump, and only gold occupied their
thoughts as we walked down the drift toward the crosscut
where the wild man was supposed to make his appearance. I
told them I had scouted for his tracks but had found no recent
sign; he probably had gone back to his hideout in the higher
country. Trying to keep them coming, I said, "If you really
want to see some fine specimens of free gold, with big chunks
of gold showing, we will go farther into the mine where I took
out the last load of high-grade. There probably is a lot more
showing in the walls and back, as well as in the face. I didn't
check up on it after we shot, just sent the Indians in to muck it
out and bring it down to the mill after the powder fumes had
aired out." Then to bring their interest to a boil, I suggested,
"We might as well get enough to take back to your friends in
New York; otherwise they won't believe you when you tell
them about your Mexican experiences." As we came to the
winze leading down to the lower level crosscut, where the
wild man would be waiting, I let them down on a rope. Their
lamps blew out in the draft, and they were in pitch darkness.
Sliding down the rope with them, I shook up the carbide in
my lamp so that it gave a good, strong light. Then I gave a
big yell, for there stood the wild man. Only a few yards from
us, he started screaming and waving his long arms.

Their wild-man hunt ended right there. We fought to get
back up the raise where the rope on which we had descended
still hung, then all ran for the portal. The rifles were where
we had left them, but the Indians that were supposed to have
waited for us had gone. We picked up the rifles and turned to
see if the wild man had followed us up the rope.

"That was damned close!" said one of the gringos, wiping the sweat from his face. "Did you see the terrible arms on that thing? He must either be a giant or a gorilla. Let's get out of here, I don't think these rifles would stop him. I would like something bigger than a thirty-thirty if we got cornered by him."

Just then we heard a yell down the slope below the mine portal and saw the wild man coming round the hill chasing some of the Indians, all yelling and screaming at the top of their voices. The wild man appeared to be gaining. I grabbed my rifle and started shooting, keeping low and well behind them so no one would get hurt. One of the New Yorkers picked up the other rifle, loaded with the ammunition I had fixed for it. He raised it and fired, but it only went "pop," and the bullet didn't travel far. He didn't notice this, however. I believe that if he had been using good ammunition he wouldn't have been able to hit anything, he was shaking so, the gun weaving around in big circles.

He soon dropped the weapon and he and his partner lit out for the desert. We didn't find them until the following day. By the time we caught up with them, they had all they wanted of Sonora, wild men, and Indians.

"How far is it to the border?" they asked. I drew them a good map and showed them how to pick up the railroad—the "iron compass" that so many of the early-day flyers used to follow before we learned navigation. It would lead them right on to Nogales.

The two New Yorkers didn't know that I could fly. They probably thought I was just a step or two ahead of the wild man, or the Indians, and that Sonora was a wild, stone-age place, as different from New York as heaven from hell.

After their ship was well gassed up and checked over, a strong wind came up, so we tied her down and went into the big adobe house, away from the sand and rock storm. These storms are not common in Sonora, as they are in Chihuahua, but when they do come in the Altar district, they are bad. Small rocks fly through the air like bullets and the dust may rise to as high as six thousand feet. I advised the gringos to sleep one more night in my home, for it would be suicide for them to try to fly in such weather. They could leave at daybreak, for these storms usually blow themselves out quickly. They could be back in the States in a couple of hours if they had good weather.

We had a fine supper and made it a farewell party with plenty of tequila for our guests. During the evening, thinking of one more joke that I could play on the two gringos, I told them a wild story of a witch who was sometimes seen in the pueblo. I said that anyone who ever saw this creature had a lot of bad trouble and that my Yaquis considered her the worst kind of bad luck.

Very early the next morning I got up and put on some old clothes that my wife had thrown away, and tied a *rebozo* around my head to make myself look as much like a witch as possible. Then I went to their plane and started the engine, warmed it up, and untied the ropes, so that I could have it airborne in only a few minutes. By the time I had everything ready, the two gringos had finished breakfast and were walking toward their ship. Before they got too close, I showed myself in the witch outfit. When they saw me, I started pushing the ship around on the ground. I ran around it several times, flapping my arms and jumping up and down. They started to run toward their ship, yelling at me to get away from it. I jumped into the cockpit and hit the electric starter. She caught right away and I took off toward them. Both lay down and tried to dig into the sand. When I was only about twenty-five feet from them, I kicked her upstairs right over their heads.

Old Pluma Negra knew about planes, for I had chased him

and the other Yaquis around like coyotes and made them dig into the dirt a time or two. I used to give them hell when I caught them out in the open while I was flying. Many times they shot at me, but they never hit anything very important. After taking off over the gringos, I kept on going until I knew they couldn't see me, behind the low hills. I then circled and flew back very low, with the engine throttled back, and landed on a good clearing about a kilometer from my house.

Both of the New York gringos were almost in tears when I came back. They told me the sad, sad story of the "old woman" who had stolen their ship, then had damn near killed them, describing "her" as very old and wild looking. She had just jumped out from behind a bush and flown the ship away, right before their eyes! They were sure that they would never see their plane again, for it had been only luck that the old woman had got it off the ground. Who would believe that anyone, among all the wild people they had seen here, especially an old Indian woman, could fly? She surely had cracked up their beautiful little ship, and probably killed herself doing it.

I pretended to be very angry with my Indians and asked them why they had allowed the old woman to fly off with the gringos' ship. They all thought it a very big joke, but none cracked a smile. I told the two gringos that they were welcome to stay with us as long as they liked; we had plenty to eat and drink and we enjoyed life a whole lot more than they could in the States. And La Ciénaga was a good place to live, as long as a man was very careful.

Before noon an Indian came in and told us that he had found an airplane, only a short distance from La Ciénaga. We all piled into one of my trucks and went to find the plane. Our New York friends again were in fine spirits, for the plane sat there in fine shape. By now the air was clear, the day beautiful, with a light tail wind blowing for their trip north. They tried to pay me for their food and lodging, but we had enjoyed their stay and all the fun we had with them too much to take anything. I gave both some raw gold and some nice specimens of tungsten ore that I had in my pockets. They said goodbye, took off, and flew north.

As for our wild man, he didn't learn to talk Yaqui to the snakes and was struck by a big rattler. My Indians fixed him up with their herbs and poultices and soon he was in fine shape again. Eventually, he became homesick for his family in the eastern part of the United States, so I gave him some money and bought him new clothes. He left Sonora, and that was the end of our wild-man fun.

One time, when we were holed up in an Indian jacal during the worst of the rainy season, El Lobo told me of one of the gully-washing rainstorms that sometimes make the parched desert of Sonora a dangerous place. It may be years between rains, but many people have been drowned in the dry arroyos when a wall of water swept down upon them. Sometimes these head rises will come roaring down the cañons and dry washes carrying large boulders, dead cattle, horses, and deer on a crest twenty feet high. Nothing can live in this deluge, which has gained volume and momentum in the mountains, miles away. There may be no sign of rain, and everything may be dry and parched when these dangerous rises occur. El Lobo asked if I had ever been in a real bad rain in the desert country. I told him of some of my own experiences with desert storms in Arizona, and asked him to tell me of the desert storms of Sonora. His story continues.

4

Desert Storm

OUNTAINS OF WATER come down out of the higher
country and all the arroyos run full of dark, muddy
water, carrying all kinds of wreckage. It may be two or three
years between these storms. I remember once we went three
years without any rain at all. When the rain does come, it
seems as though all the water in the world has been dumped
on the desert. I remember one time when I was driving an old
army truck I had bought at an auction in California. It had
ten wheels and three differentials and was equipped with a
good winch. Often I would buy these trucks and, after getting
my use out of them, sell them for as much as or more than
they had cost me.

All the washes and arroyos that were normally dry were

running bank full. A lot of them were real rivers for a while. A truck like mine was the only vehicle that could get through at such times. I often hauled the mail during these storms, as the buses would be stuck along the route.

On this particular trip I had a load of ore, with mail and people piled all over the truck. The fenders as well as the box of the truck were loaded to capacity. These people had been marooned for several days in buses that had been stuck since the storm started. All kinds of people—bankers, businessmen, women, and kids, and the Lord only knows who else, were riding with me. I picked up everyone who was stranded that could possibly find a place to hang on. I had been forced to leave at least as many more behind, promising to come back for them after I had unloaded.

The old army truck made its way through the roaring washes and was often mired down. When this happened, I sent out a winch line with my Yaquis and they would dig a deep pit and bury a timber "deadman" that I carried for this purpose. I would throw the winch into gear and out the big rig would come, shaking herself loose from the mud and water. Some of these washes were running over three feet deep and often had water over their banks, but the engine on the high old Autocar never drowned out. This vehicle sat high above the ground and I could go just about anywhere I wished in it. This was one of the finest vehicles I ever used for desert travel.

Our trip through the desert in the storm was like a big picnic and lots of fun. Everyone was happy to be on his way again after having been stranded in all kinds of vehicles. In one of the widest and deepest arroyos on our route we found a nearly new Cadillac stalled with the water about half way up to its top. It had gone as far as the middle of the stream before drowning out early in the storm, and the water had risen so high that the people in it had been forced to climb up on the top to keep from being carried away. The water was running into the upstream doors and out the downstream. This was all that had saved it and the people from being swept away in the swift current. The driver and the other occupants, from Hermosillo, had been stranded two days by the time we came along. They called to us for help. They were really desperate and offered to pay me well if I could save them and their car.

I told them that I didn't want any pay; I was having a good time and enjoyed being out in the storm. I just told them, "Hell, put your money away, I don't need it. Here, have a shot of *bacanora* to keep you from catching cold." Good old *bacanora*, tastes like kerosene or gasoline but has a kick like a whole herd of mules.

I had one of my Yaquis toss a log chain to them and told them to fasten it well to the frame of the car. The water was running fast and deep, and small trees, brush and even large rocks were being swept down by the current. The mess coming down the arroyo was topped by thick, dirty foam, like frosting on a chocolate cake.

The people on top of the car, afraid of getting in the water, fastened the chain to the bumper instead of the frame. I told them that as deep as they were stuck in the muddy bottom of the stream the bumper wouldn't stand the strain. They'd better get a little wetter and fasten it where I told them. They thought that because it was a big, wide bumper it should hold, and told me to go ahead and lay into it with the truck.

"Okay," I said, "it is your car, go ahead and put the chain wherever you wish; hold the damn thing in your teeth if you want to. I will start out very slowly and carefully. Give me the word whenever you are ready."

Pretty soon they yelled, "¡*Vámonos!*" I eased in the clutch and gently fed gas to the old Autocar. It leaned on the chain like a small locomotive, which it almost was, and the entire bumper and about half the grill came out in one piece. There was a terrible crying and wringing of hands by the owner, for car repairs are expensive in Mexico, besides being hard to get.

We did accomplish something, however, for through the big hole where the grill had been it was now a simple matter to get to the frame and fasten the chain where it should have been hooked the first time. When I again put the truck in gear, she gurgled and groaned, and out came the car.

On we drove through the endless washes and arroyos. After hours of this, still towing the Cadillac, we came to another car stuck in the middle of another deep wash. This time it was a new Studebaker, and we soon had the lighter car out of the water and tied on behind the other. We made quite a procession, but the old truck just took it all in stride. Finally we got to Santa Ana with the whole outfit. I got rid of my passengers and unloaded my ore at a siding near the railroad depot. The wealthy city Mexicans looked almost as bad as my Yaquis in their muddy, ruined clothes, but all were happy to be safe.

5

Don Teodoro's Ghost

IKE MOST SIMPLE FOLK of limited education, *campesinos* [rural peasants] believe in all sorts of things. They usually are very superstitious. *Brujos, brujas,* and *bultos* [male and female witches and ghosts] are quite real to them. Wherever one may go in Latin America, wild tales of the powers of these supernatural beings may be heard, and they are believed implicitly.

When I lived at La Ciénaga, which is little more than a ghost mining camp since the revolution, I owned the big *casa* of which I have told you. In it was my home and the home of many of Puñalita's numerous relatives. It also housed a small hotel, my miners' bar, a big *bodega* [warehouse] where I stored supplies for the mine, machinery and parts, a good repair and machine shop, assay office, and a large courtyard where I kept my trucks. We also had the ghost of the old Spanish miner to contend with, but he didn't bother us very often.

I kept the bar just for my miners so that they could buy any kind of liquor for just enough above wholesale cost to pay the wages of the *cantinero*. Vaqueros, and anyone else besides miners, had to pay plenty for liquor at my little private cantina. My little cantina was the gathering place for all the miners and prospectors in that area, and my *cantinero* was a good bartender and a nice fellow. He was worth every bit of the fifteen pesos a day I paid him, and probably didn't steal much more than his wages.

There were a few large cattle ranches and several smaller ones from fifteen to fifty miles from La Ciénaga, and my cantina was the nearest and most convenient for the ranchers and their vaqueros. Often a vaquero would see the lights from far out on the desert and would come in for a few drinks and perhaps a good fight with my miners. Sometimes they would drive a few cows in and make a deal with the *cantinero* for liquor in exchange for the cattle. They would say to him, "Here are two good steers, how long can we stay drunk for them?"

The *cantinero* would call in a few miners and prospectors, and they would make up a pot to buy the steers for meat. The vaqueros would proceed with their drunk. Theirs was not a wholesale drunk, like the miners, for they had to pay full price for their liquor, and then some if the *cantinero* didn't like them. He would always tell them, "This is a *gambusino* bar, for miners and prospectors, and we do not care to sell drinks to vaqueros."

Our little ranchero and vaquero trade kept us in fresh meat, so we tolerated them and made a little profit so we could have a party every once in a while without much cost. Every *gam-*

busino in the district would travel miles across the hot desert to our fiestas, which sometimes lasted for days.

One time some vaqueros came to the cantina at just about dark of a cold and windy evening—a very fine evening for the ghost of Don Teodoro Salazar to come to your house and ask for food. It is on such nights that he rides his big, black horse into La Ciénaga, in his fancy clothes of a Spanish grandee of a couple hundred years ago and does penance for his cruelty to the Indian miners who were his slaves when he was alive. All of the Mexican and Indian houses were closed up tight with all the windows and doors barred on nights such as this, for no one had any desire to speak to old Don Teodoro, said to be buried deep in the workings of the haunted Mina Teodorina that I had been cleaning out in preparation for re-opening it. In the Yaqui uprising against their Spanish lords,[10] he had been done in by the great-great grandfathers of my Yaquis, and there he should stay and not wander around on windy nights. He usually did, except on nights such as this, which would draw him back to our little pueblo of La Ciénaga. He would go from door to door, asking for food, and everyone was very much afraid of his ghost, although he never harmed anyone so far as I could learn.

The little cantina was lighted brightly and the radio was going full blast, for we never shut down the mill generator, which furnished electricity for the town. A few miners were drinking and talking, as were a small group of vaqueros who had traded beef for drinks earlier in the day. One of the miners remarked that this was a night that old Don Teodoro would be abroad on his quest for food. A big argument started right away between the miners and vaqueros about

[10] The Yaqui uprising of 1740 occurred in the Mayo and Yaqui country farther south. As previously noted, the destruction related here may have been a part of the Pima revolt of 1751, with Yaqui slaves participating.

ghosts. The vaqueros claimed that the people of La Ciénaga were cowards. As for themselves, they didn't believe in ghosts of long-dead miners and were not afraid of the biggest ghost we could show them. This led to some bets being laid, and a big pot was raised among the miners to match the vaqueros' bet. The vaqueros wagered that one of them could go to the cemetery, where the body of an old dry placer miner had been buried about two weeks before, and return unharmed.

The *camposanto*, a quarter of a mile northeast of town, was quite old. Many Spanish miners and their families were buried there in large, once-beautiful graves and tombs, now in ruins. The bet laid was that one of the vaqueros would not have the courage to go to the cemetery alone on this stormy night and drive a large new nail with a cross mark filed on its head into the new wooden cross over the recent burial. The bartender found a suitable nail, and the identifying marks were filed. A young, loud-mouthed vaquero said that he was not afraid of man, beast, or ghost and would take the nail out to the grave and drive it wherever they wanted it. He took the nail, had another glass of tequila, and rode off at a gallop toward the cemetery. Each group had given the bartender a hundred pesos to hold for the winners.

Those left in the cantina continued their drinking and talking, but the young vaquero did not return. At last it was decided that he had lost his nerve and ridden back to his rancho, and the wager was paid to the miners and prospectors. Next day the poor vaquero was found hanging from the cross at the grave of the old miner, dead. He had driven the nail into the cross according to the terms of the bet but, as a result of the strong wind, had driven it through the sleeve of his coat. Finding himself held to the cross by some unseen and unknown force, he apparently had died of fright.

Indians and Mexicans are fatalists. Sometimes they decide that they should die and just lie down and do it. An otherwise healthy, intelligent Indian, on learning that someone has paid a *brujo* for a charm to bring about his death for some injury to the other person, often will just lie down and die in a few days' time. This fellow had no marks on him, so we knew that none of the miners was responsible. When he found that he couldn't get away from the grave, the shock and fright must have killed him. It was not a sight soon to be forgotten, the poor fellow hanging there in the chilly dawn, his face twisted with fear.

A new ghost was added to those already wandering around La Ciénaga.

My Yaqui wife, Puñalita, was always afraid of the old Spanish mine owner's ghost, as were all the Indians and Mexicans around La Ciénaga. Old Don Teodoro had almost as many people scared of him after being dead a couple of hundred years as when he still lived. The story told among the *habitantes* is that when the wind blows in the evening and the sun is just setting, the don comes home from his mine. He is always supposed to come to my big, sprawling *casa*, for it was his home when he was alive. He is finely dressed and rides a big, powerful black horse with a high, ornate silver-mounted saddle of the old Spanish style no longer seen. Many people at La Ciénaga claim they have seen and talked to Don Teodoro during one of his many visits to the pueblo. It is said that he goes from house to house in the village, asking to buy food. He does not beg. The Yaquis say that he does not rest well, deep in his old mine where his body was consigned by his Indian slaves when they rebelled at his cruelty.

One evening when I came home from the mine, Puñalita and her sister had quite a story to tell. Having prepared the evening meal, they were waiting for me, listening for the sound of the big truck, which I had driven up to the mine. There was a knock at the door, and both went to see who had

come to visit. My wife's numerous Yaqui relatives were frequent visitors, and they thought that it might be some of them. Instead they found a stranger, a big, tall man dressed in a fine red coat and high black boots, with a wide belt, a big sword, and a tall hat with feathers in it. She thought that he might be a wealthy cattleman on his way to some fiesta or one of my friends, not of her acquaintance, who had come dressed this way as a joke.

The man looked real. She didn't think of his being a ghost, for he looked to be as much flesh and blood as anyone she had ever seen. He asked the two women, in fine Spanish, if he might buy some food, for he had traveled far since he had last eaten and had great hunger. He seemed such a polite gentleman that she invited him into the house and told him to sit at the table while she and her sister went into the *cocina* to get the food. When they returned to the dining room, he was gone.

They went to the door to see if his big black horse with the fine silver-mounted saddle was still tied where he had left it, just outside the door. The horse, too, was gone, and they could find no tracks where it had stood. They then realized that this was no man, as he had appeared to be, but must surely be the ghost of Don Teodoro.

The two women were very much afraid and were as near being hysterical as an Indian woman can be by the time I arrived. But Don Teodoro Salazar apparently does not bring bad luck and never harms those he visits, as it is claimed so many of the old Spanish ghosts do when they come back to haunt the places they knew in life. His old mine is said to be haunted, too, but I spent a long time working it and, although we did find many human bones in the shaft, which the Yaqui had filled after killing the Spaniards, I never saw or heard any ghosts. Nor did I ever see Don Teodoro. Maybe he visits only Mexicans and Indians. *¿Quién sabe?*

6

The Haunted Church

THERE IS A HAUNTED CHURCH about twelve miles south of Caborca. It belonged to one of the first missions founded by Padre Eusebio Kino in the string of missions extending from Sonora into Arizona.[11] On this old church is a bronze plate that tells of the time some gringos from Alta California sailed in a large ship from San Francisco into the Mar de Cortés, also called the Gulf of California. These gringos took the town of La Paz in Baja California and then sailed to Sonora and marched inland to Caborca and the nearby

[11] Under Father Kino's leadership, the Jesuits entered Sonora in 1687. Kino established a frontier mission station at Cucurpe, in the San Miguel River valley, then founded Mission Dolores, fifteen miles up the San Miguel, as headquarters. By 1695 Kino had established a chain of missions along the Altar and Magdalena rivers, including the one at Caborca.

gold mines. There probably were about two hundred of these tough gringo filibusters, all of them armed. They were mostly miners and prospectors from the California gold fields who had heard of the rich mines of Sonora and attempted to take them.[12]

After taking Caborca, the gringos stole all the good looking women they could catch in Caborca and the surrounding country. They took the women to the mission winery, a long bowshot from the church, and soon a wild party was in progress.

Among the defenders of Caborca were some Yaquis and Mexicans who had escaped the massacre and retreated to the church. They had successfully resisted every attack against this strong position, and could hold out until lack of food and water forced them to capitulate. The old church has walls eight feet thick. The roof and high bell towers provided such excellent protection that they had been able to stand off several wild attempts to dislodge them. After each attack, the gringos returned to their drunken carousal. The party continued for several days with the good priests' barrels of fine wines, but the invaders kept close watch on the church, so none of the defenders might escape.

In a desperate attempt to dislodge the enemy, the Yaquis

[12] The Yaquis through the years have been victimized by many filibusters of different nationalities. Reference here is to Colonel William Walker's expedition in 1854. Eluding U.S. authorities who desired to stop the undertaking, he left California with forty-eight men and landed at La Paz, where he recruited two hundred Mexican reinforcements to help him establish the Republic of Lower California with himself as president. He quickly abandoned this plan, however, in favor of a larger one: the Republic of Sonora, including Baja California. As he moved into Sonora, Walker's ranks were riddled by desertion, and he was left with only a hundred men. By the time he got out of Mexico, only thirty-five remained, possibly a tribute to the Yaqui resistance at Caborca.

in the church made fire arrows of hollow reeds filled with some incendiary material that smolders for a while, then bursts into hot flame, and their best bowmen shot these missiles into the winery's thatched roof. Before the gringos realized their dangerous position, the roof was a mass of flames. The thick, tinder-dry thatch could not be quenched, and those inside who were not too drunk ran out, leaving most of their weapons and ammunition behind. Without spare ammunition and with many of their number unarmed and too drunk to fight, all those not killed by the Yaquis and Mexicans were driven off into the desert. My Yaqui relatives, who told me this story, showed me such fire arrows and how they were used.

The same story, very much as I had heard it from the descendants of the victorious native forces, is written on the bronze plate on the wall of the church ruins. When I lived in Sonora, the church had been abandoned for many years. The Río Magdalena passes near it, and when it floods, which it does about every three or four years, it takes a little more of the old mission church. The heavy rains and cloudbursts in the Sierra Madre, and in the lower ranges to the west, send big walls of water down the river, causing great floods that sometimes tear up the desert below. The village that had grown up around the old mission was the original town of Caborca, but because of the floods it was moved to its present location, ten or twelve miles north. All that is left of old Caborca is the church ruins and a few low walls where the mission and the houses once stood. Several small treasures have been found here.

One night Puñalita and I were at our cantina, talking to a group of gringo prospectors who had drifted in that day. I had bought a round of drinks for everyone, and had given them some information about the location of some old mines they were interested in. We talked of prospecting and treasure hunting in Mexico, and the talk got around to the ghosts that are supposed to guard many of the ancient treasures of Latin America. The supernatural is a common subject among the Mexicans who prospect or mine, and most of the people of the rural areas. We had several active ghosts right there in La Ciénaga, according to those who should know, so the strangers must be told all about them and others in the district.

The bartender mentioned that the ancient Spanish church in the old town of Caborca was full of ghosts and had been haunted ever since the Indians revolted, almost two hundred years before. All of the priests and nuns had been massacred, as had the tame mission Indians.[13] The gringos just laughed when he told them this, and said that they did not believe in ghosts. They said that ghosts were only in the minds of over-imaginative and superstitious people who didn't have anything else to think about. The bartender was a firm believer, however, and did not like to be called ignorant and superstitious by a bunch of gringos who had just popped up out of the desert to laugh at things they didn't know anything about. He slapped a thousand pesos on the bar and said that he would bet it against any man who would stay in the old

[13] In March and April, 1685, the Pimas of the Altar valley rose in revolt. Father Francisco Xavier Saeta and several servants were slain at the Caborca mission. The mission church was burned, the livestock killed or stampeded. Similar depredations were noted at several neighboring missions along the Magdalena and Altar valleys. In the Pima uprising of 1751, more than one hundred Spaniards lost their lives, including the Jesuits at Caborca and Sonóita. Mines, ranches, and missions were abandoned. When the Marqués de Rubí made his frontier inspection in 1767, the Caborca mission had sixty Indian families and was administered by a single Jesuit missionary. In the Royal Regulations of 1772, reference is made to "the old mission of Caborca, which was destroyed by the Apaches."

church overnight. It was believed that no man could stay in the church alone until sunrise and live.

One of the gringos said, "I would like to take you up on that bet, but if we fool around here another day it will make us just that much later getting a start at prospecting. I wouldn't fool around for just a thousand peso bet, but if you want to make it five hundred U.S. dollars, I will take you up. I warn you, however, if you do make the bet, I sure intend to win your money."

The bartender turned to me and asked if I would go fifty-fifty with him on the bet, for he didn't have that much money. "Then, too," he said, "maybe the old priests and their dead nuns will not work tonight. *¿Quién sabe?* I do not have all of the money to pay if I should lose."

I told him that I would lose half of the bet gladly if there really were ghosts in the old church and the gringo had guts enough to hold out against them all night. I knew how scary the old, abandoned town could be in the moonlight, and I was pretty sure that no one would stay in the old church alone for a full night. We went to the other cantina and put up our wagers with the bartender there. He would pay off the winners when we returned from the church the next day. The news of the crazy bet quickly made the rounds in the little town and soon about twenty other *gambusinos* and miners, with a few cattlemen and cotton farmers, turned out to see the fun.

We started for the abandoned church in two of my dump trucks, loaded to the guards, and soon arrived at the ruined village with its lonely ruins. Even though I knew what a lonely place it would be at night, I could see this was a rough, tough gringo, and he just might stay until morning. We all wanted to be there when and if he came out of the church at sunrise. Fun is fun, so we had planned a fine time and brought several cases of beer and a lot of steaks to broil. My father-in-law, Pluma Negra, had come with us. None of our party was armed except the gringo who was to stay in the church.

He had his machete and a good thirty-thirty and two full boxes of ammo. He was prepared to put up a good fight if he had to. He told us, "Now, fellows, I am a good sport and I like to have fun, but no funny stuff tonight. If anyone comes into the old church to try to scare me, I will shoot, and I do mean business."

We all told him that we were his friends and that he need not hold his fire, for none of us would bother him. We would just go ahead with our little party right where we were and wait for him to come out when the sun came up.

All of us went into the old church while he fixed his bedroll and got comfortable. Leaving him a few bottles of beer, we shut the big, heavy old doors behind us.

About a hundred yards from the church we built a good fire. By the time it had burned down to hot coals, we were all hungry again, so we broiled the rest of the steaks and drank beer and told tall stories—mostly about ghosts. No one slept; we all sat around the fire until the east began to show the first light of dawn. We decided that our five hundred dollars was as good as lost, and we were all cold and maybe a little drunk. Suddenly we heard a terrific banging on the big doors, and out came the gringo in high gear. He had no rifle, hat or boots and was screaming at the top of his voice and frothing at the mouth.

We all ran toward him, asking what had happened, but he could not talk. He ran as though all the devils of hell were breathing down his neck. Still screaming, he ran toward the fire, and kept right on running through the hot coals, barefoot.

We decided that he must be either drunk or plumb loco, so we caught him and held him down. He had gone completely

mad. We took him to the little hotel in Caborca and put him to bed. He flung himself around so badly that we were afraid he would injure himself, still trying to run from whatever had put him into this terrible condition. We had to tie him down. We got the Mexican doctor to look at him, and he gave him some morphine to quiet him. Finally he stopped struggling and went to sleep. Completely out of his head the next two days, he was much improved by the afternoon of the third day. But he still was a very sick man. We did not keep his five hundred dollars, for we all felt very badly about the way that night had turned out.

At last he was well enough to tell us what had happened to bring him to this terrible condition. He told us he didn't know how long he had been asleep, but that he had drunk a bottle of beer and settled down for the night. He had no trouble getting to sleep, but something had caused him to awaken suddenly, he didn't know what.

The old church was bathed in some kind of soft light, as though dim moonlight were shining in. There was no moon to speak of, however, and the entire church was filled with this dull light, not just moonpaths from the high windows. Whatever the light source, he could make out details of the church interior quite well. At first he thought we had come with torches to see how he was getting along. But when he turned to look for us, we were, of course, not there. What he did see was enough to make him forget everything else.

Standing before him were about fifty nuns, all bleeding and many badly hacked up, as though with sharp machetes. Some had no arms; others bled profusely from cuts about the head, and all bore terrible wounds. They appeared to be singing a mass. A soft, deep music seemed to fill the church, a sound that he seemed to feel, rather than hear, in the ordinary sense of hearing.

He still had no fear, for he believed that we had put on

outlandish makeup to frighten him. He did not use his rifle, as he had threatened; yet he was the sort of gringo that you knew would shoot—not the type to make idle threats.

While the nuns sang, a tall priest approached him from a door at the side of the church, perhaps the sacristy. The priest, covered with blood, had been decapitated and carried his head in his hands. While the gringo watched the ghastly scene, completely fascinated and without fear, an unseen force jerked him violently from behind, pulling him out of his bedroll. Whatever had hold of him started to drag him along the church floor, toward the altar. Struggling free, he ran screaming from the church.

I think perhaps the Indians and Mexicans may be right in believing the old, old church, where so many innocent people have been cruelly murdered, to be full of ghosts and dangerous.

Anyone who wishes to do so may sleep there, but I don't like the way things there feel to me, even in broad daylight. The Indians have told me many times that a rich treasure is hidden somewhere about it—far more than has been found so far—but I do not care to go there and look. I may be a big coward, but when I go near this place, the short hair on the back of my neck rises. That's warning enough for me.

PART TWO

Generals, Gold, and Idols

*While we were associated in some mining ventures in south-
ern Mexico, I learned more of El Lobo's life and experiences
as a flier and soldier of fortune in numerous Latin American
revolutions. He had been associated with many of the colorful
and ruthless generals of Latin American republics who for so
long called the shots in the shooting politics of their countries. I had been curious about his long association with one
of these generals, whom I also had known slightly many years
before I had met El Lobo. Knowing that they had been more
like father and son than business associates, I asked Ricardo
to tell me of his experiences with the man. The pace is slow
in Latin America, and there is time to remember and relate
past experiences. His story of an episode that happened some
thirty-five years ago, as he related it to me about fifteen years
later, follows.*

7

The Old General

MY OLD GENERAL[1] WOULD SAY, "My friend, we have
many fine things in our hands. If we work with care,
we shall become very rich men again. There are many people
who do not care for me very much; also, there are people
who would die for me. Some people are very narrow in their
heads, as you know, and, over a few thousand head of cattle,
they will shoot a man—even a general! I am not a bad fellow
and I do not ever steal cattle for pleasure or to buy things for
myself. All the cows they say I took in the north, and also

---

[1] The general must not be identified. Not only was he of a prominent
military family, some of whom have rendered noteworthy service to
Mexico in the past, but also his descendants still are active in affairs
of the country.

maybe some in the south, I took only to feed my men, and always gave the proper requisition if I could find the owner and if he still happened to be alive. Of course there were times that there were extra cows that we could not eat, all at once. These extra cattle I sold to people because I needed money to pay my men and also to run my army, but people do not always look at my past in a nice way. They say '¡*Mira*! There goes that fat *bandido* general who stole my family's cows. Then they reach for their *pistola*—but then their hand gets a little weak, because they remember that the first slug will not stop me. They know that I am still pure steel and that I will turn and send them to hell before I die!''

That is the way the old general would talk to me about his past. Often he would refight a battle with Zapata or Villa or Salgado in a cantina in some little town where we had landed after coming out of the mountains from a prospecting trip. We would go to the best restaurant in town, sit at the best table, and order the finest dinner, with a bottle of the best Scotch whiskey or other expensive liquor. Often he would drink a couple of bottles at one sitting, for he thought nothing of pouring out a waterglass full of rum, whiskey, or other liquor and drinking it down just to clear the dust from his throat. After three or four steaks, *carne asada*, he would say, "This is a nice little town. I like this place, my boy; see what pretty girls are here and what good figures they have. They cook the meat well here, and the *frijoles refritos* are as good as those my own wife fixes. If the mines we have looked at are as good as the old records say they are, this is where we will stay and make our homes."

Then I would say in English, "But, General! We have only about twenty pesos left—and the train fare, and the rent of the mules, and——." "Never mind, my boy. Drink up! There is still good whiskey left in the bottle. I will borrow money from the man who owns this place. He will lend money to a general, I am sure. I will sign for everything, for you know that I am still a general and the bill will be paid by the secretary of war in Mexico, D.F. Old General Olacharo is my friend and he okays all bills that I sign. I have also found out that the passenger train will not come until late tonight, so we will use the switch engine and the caboose that stands over there on the siding. She will take us to Mexico ahead of the passenger train. While you were shaving and taking a bath, I spoke to the yardmaster. He is a very old friend of mine, once a capitan under my command, so he will clear the line for us. He said, 'We will take a few drinks for the boys in the caboose and the engine crew, and go right into Mexico for old time's sake.'

"We will be in Mexico by daylight if the engine does not choose to go off the tracks or explode. The railroad is all grades and curves from here to Mexico, so the little switch engine with its little wheels may do her work better than the long-legged engine with her long train of Pullmans. I will sleep in the caboose and you may ride in the engine, as I have told him and his crew that you are a fine locomotive engineer and that your family once owned a railroad."

It was a wonderful life that I lived with the old general. He and some of the other powerful old generals have been very close to me. He told me, "You assay and prospect and fly for us, and we will back you. We must always back each other, for there are few of us old generals of the revolution left, and we must show everyone that we are still generals. If our enemies believe us weak, we have but little time left to live."

Some of his associates still say of me, "He may not be a gringo, for many people say he is one of old General X's bastard sons." I am not the general's bastard son, but many Mexicans believe that I am. All of the old generals had a lot of extra sons, and if you are a favorite son, bastard or not, you are well set. The story got started in this way. One time when the general and I wrecked our airplane we went to the cantina in a little town to get out of the rain and see how badly we were cut up. We had walked through mud and brush for several miles and looked pretty bad when we arrived. The general ordered a bottle of Scotch, and began figuring out our next move. He was not in uniform, and three guides who had stopped to get out of the heavy rain with their parties of tourists thought that he was a fat *norteamericano* tourist and that I was his son. He was pure Spanish with no Indian blood at all, with very fair skin and blue eyes—like our friend, his brother, but heavier.

The guides were a little drunk and they came over to our table and helped themselves to the general's whiskey and said, "Why don't you and your father come with us? We know all of Mexico and can show you many fine things. We have a car and will work cheap for you." The one who made the pitch helped himself to another drink from the general's bottle.

The general said to him, "Look here, boy, I am a general and I don't need a guide in Mexico. Stay away from me and stay away from my whiskey."

The fool guide said, "A general? What kind of a general?" Then he said in Spanish, "You look like a fat, dumb gringo to me." Then he took another big shot of the general's Scotch.

The general was a big man and, although he looked fat, he was well muscled and strong. His biceps were large and he was much harder than he appeared to be, for all his years and old wounds. He has *muy hombre* in any man's language. He picked the guide up by the throat with one hand and threw him behind the bar, then hit his two friends so quickly that I didn't see it happen—just saw them sprawled on the floor, dead to the world. Then he said, very softly, "What kind of a general, you ask? A *cavalry* general! What else would you like to know?"

The place had become very quiet. No one moved, or even seemed to breathe. The *cantinero* said, "General, would you and your son care for another drink?" We, of course, never turned down such an invitation and were served another of the finest in the house.

The general took a sip and said, "My boy, this is a very nice place, is it not? I never shoot people in a nice place like this if I can help it. A shooting always spoils the atmosphere of a cantina. Is it not so? I wish to rest a while now, for I believe that when I went through the windshield of our pretty little airplane, my shoulder was hurt."

Whenever the general was near a railroad station, he would use a train—passenger, freight, or switch engine—or even a handcar. Of course most of the railroads in Mexico run through steep mountains with many curves and difficult grades. Often the equipment and the roadbed and bridges are not very good, for now that everything has been nationalized things are done the Mexican way, if they get done at all. The patron saints of all railroaders must work overtime around the clock in Mexico.

Once, when coming out of the mountains after several weeks of prospecting, we came to a railroad track in the hills. There was a section gang working near by, and the old man said, "My boy, this track runs to the town of Colonia, not far from here. On the mules we will be two days and a half getting there, but on the rails it is only a few hours. We will go by rail, for I am tired of Indian food and thirsty for some good liquor." He turned to our major domo and said to him, "Have your Indians take the mules and all my equipment to Hotel Salía in Colonia and be very sure that you do not lose or spoil anything."

They all grinned and said, "*Sí, sí, mi general.*" Then he said to the section foreman, "Get that goddam handcar on the rails and take me to Colonia. Load those *bolsas* of ore on and be careful of them." Pointing his finger at the section boss, he said, "Get on! We may need you." And to me he said, "Run the car, I don't trust these Indians with machines." He got on the car and settled himself on some serapes, pulled down his general's cap with the big gold eagle and the two silver stars and said, "Well, what is holding us?"

The section foreman sputtered and looked at his watch. He tried to say something, but the general didn't give him a chance to get any words out of his mouth. He just said, "I know you have to finish fixing the track, but never mind that now; it can wait until you come back. Just get this thing started down the track to Colonia, or would you rather that I shoot you now?"

The section foreman looked at his watch again and tried to speak, but looked at the general's military cap and the big frontier model Colt forty-five on his hip, shrugged, and shut up. He crossed himself and prayed, and I could see that he was anything but happy about the whole affair.

"Let her fly, my boy," said the general; "I like to feel the cool wind on my face."

Let her fly I did. Around the curves we went with the little Fairmont steaming and a stream of fire flying from the exhaust. The rail joints clicked and the flanges screamed as we took the curves while the general smiled through his clenched teeth. Then, far off, I heard a whistle, faint but clear in the high mountain air. The section foreman turned pale, then sort of blue, and crossed himself again. He tried to say something, but was so scared he couldn't get any words out. At last he managed to cry, "¡*Ese es el rápido*!" The fast passenger train, which he had been trying to warn us of all the time. "It is the whistle of the fast one."

"Well!" said the general, as though it was all the fault of the poor Indian. "Goddam you, you stupid Indian *pinche buey* [ox], why did you not speak of this El Rápido? Do you wish to wreck us and have all of us killed for your stupidity? For your foolishness and poor judgment I will execute you. Yes, as soon as I can find time I surely will execute you."

I had cut the switch as soon as I heard the whistle and shut off the gasoline and set the hand brakes. The section foreman was dropping sand on the rail to help stop the flying handcar. With the engine shut off we could hear the exhausts of the two engines on the fast passenger—and damned close, too. Out of a cut below us came the passenger engines. They looked big and dangerous with the steam from their air pumps and safety valves trailing over their boilers and gray-black smoke gushing from their short stacks.

"*¡Caramba!*" said the general, "It is El Rápido; does she not look pretty coming up the hill?" He calmly lighted a cigar as we finally slowed to a stop. We had scarcely wrestled the handcar off the tracks when El Rápido stormed by as though we did not exist. "What a nice train," the general remarked. "If we were in the dining car, we could get some watermelon and ice cream and some whiskey and good frijoles. What a pretty train it is!"

The poor section foreman had collapsed as soon as we had the handcar off the track, and now the general shook him with his boot and said, "Well! This is not Sunday afternoon and we are not in church! Get this goddam car back on the track and let us go to the city!"

The poor Indian cried, "*¡No! ¡No, mi general!* I will go back to town, God willing."

I had about had enough of meeting flyers on blind curves along the track, so I said, "*Mi general*, ask this poor ox in his own tongue if there are any more trains following El Rápido, for he must be made to understand us if we are not to be killed. He will know what will be coming by, for he was working on the track and must know the schedule." Schedules do not mean too much on most Mexican lines, but I did not wish to hurt the old man's feelings by saying so.

He said to the section foreman, "Well, Indian son of a dog, you tried to wreck me!"

The poor Indian denied this and said that he had done everything he could to warn us, but that we had not allowed him to speak.

"What comes next on the track, do you know, fool, or not?"

He took off his hat and said, "*Sí, sí, mi general*, next comes two freight trains. We will go now through two tunnels and then come to the town of Cristo del Pino. In Cristo del Pino, with your permission, *mi general*, we will stop and by the telegraph wire we shall know where these two trains are. God may not be looking our way when the freight trains come and it will be well to know where they are."

Down the long winding track and through the smoke filled tunnels we flew, with the section foreman crouched down behind the general and the little Fairmont car flying like a yellow bird down the winding rails. ¡*Viva México*! What a life! Life with a Latin American general is a lot of fun, but there are times when things get a little rough and you wish that you had been a good boy, done as people had asked you to, and settled down as a man of means and taken care of what you had at home. As the story goes:

> The years go by and you wonder why
>   You left your home to roam,
> Away down there in that tropic air,
>   Away down there alone.
> For there's a one-way track
>   And it don't lead back,
> Way down in Mexico.
>   You may find me there

> Or any old where
>> That a tumbleweed may go.
> I'm off for a trip,
>> Don't need no grip.
> I'm taking one more ride,
>> Away down there in the tropic air.
> It must be in my hide.
>> So clackety clack says the main line track
> You'll never get back—never get back.

So the old song of the Tropical Tramp goes, and it is pretty nearly right. You never get back, once you have drunk of the Chagres water[2] and of the mango eaten free, you must leave the beaten track and you will come back—back to the land of the coconut tree.

[2] Water from the Chagres River, Panama.

8

The *Coronela's* Gold

THE OLD GENERAL had stopped to rest the Indians and pack mules, high up on the trail near the summit of San Francisco Mountain. The road that now allows the traveler to drive his car through these rough mountains of southern Mexico had not then been completed. Only a few horse and mule trails, following those of the pre-Columbian Indians, allowed access to the ranches and mines from the east, the way we had come. Our pack train, managed by several *mozos* [servants] was strung out in a long line behind us, happy for this chance to rest and breathe after the hard climb in the thin mountain air. High up on the mountain, the air was so clear that we could see for many miles. It is a beautiful country, the mountains of southern Mexico, and I never tire of the vista from its high places.

My companion raised his arm and pointed off in the distance. "Do you see that spot out there on the plain, where the ground is whiter than in other places?" he asked. "That is Sochechalpa. In this pueblo lives a colonel who once served with me during the revolution. For many years I thought this colonel was a man, a very fine soldier, but later I was told that *mi coronel* was a woman. Her name is Robles, and she came to me with several hundred well-armed and mounted Indians.

"This *coronela* writes to me that she has a rancho of many thousand hectares and many thousand cattle. On this rancho is a gold mine that has not been worked for many, many years—maybe not since the time of the French, or even before that. The colonel would like to have us examine this old mine and, if it is a good prospect, to have us work it."

I told him that this sounded interesting and, as the *mozos* and animals should have rested enough, we should get started if we were to get there before night.

The general grinned and said, "Yes, the colonel has a fine, big house and plenty of good meat to eat. This is a fine time for us to go to look at the little gold mine, for we are broke and have many Indians to feed. Let us get started at once so that we may find good food tonight and not have to eat the terrible cooking of that Indian who claims to be a good *cocinero*, all the while trying to poison us with the food he cooks."

Off we rode, toward the little village far below the plain. Just as darkness was falling, we arrived at the pueblo, tired, dusty and thirsty from long hours in the saddle. Having taken the shortest route, we entered the town on a narrow side street with small adobe houses on both sides. It was a typical mountain village of the dry plains, not quite desert, but with few trees and they all dry and dust-covered. Not a soul could we see; the town seemed deserted. This was unusual at that time of day, for there ordinarily would be women carrying water from the well and men loafing in doorways, watching the strangers riding in.

Riding on, we came upon a vaquero lying in a pool of blood in the middle of the dirt street. I dismounted and rolled the fellow over and listened for a heartbeat. There was none. I opened his shirt and found a bullet hole just under his heart.

"Shot!" said the general. "And very dead, too! Leave him there and we will send someone to take care of him after we have had a few drinks."

Continuing on toward the center of town, we soon found another dead vaquero. He too had been shot, and was sprawled in the doorway of an adobe house. "Goddam!" said the general. "What kind of business goes on here? Let us go to the cantina and find out."

On the floor of the cantina we found three more dead men, badly shot up. The *cantinero* was nowhere to be found. "Hell," said the general, "this is a bad thing! Let us have a little drink. Pour me some of that mescal back there, the Gusano del Oro;[3] it seems to be the best they have. After we have had a drink or two we will go to the home of Colonel Robles and find out what the hell goes on in this place."

The village seemed as a dead town of the ancient ones. No one stirred anywhere. Whenever a small war starts in the mountain or desert towns in Mexico, all the good people bar their doors and windows and let the others shoot it out. The peaceful citizens of Sochechalpa were all in hiding. They had no intention of catching a wild bullet. It was now quite dark, so we lighted the oil lamps in the cantina and had a few more drinks. Still no one came, so we started for the house of Colonel Robles.

Approaching the house, we could hear a small electric light plant, and the big house was lighted as though for a party. We turned our mounts over to the Indians, who were

[3] A brand of mescal, which has a maguey worm in the bottle. The name means "golden worm."

clustered together, probably from fear of the dead men they had seen, or of joining them. The general swaggered up to the great door and rapped long and loud. Then he shouted, "Colonel! Colonel Robles! It is your old general! Let us in!" The door opened and there stood a short, dark complexioned man. At least it looked like a man to me. The colonel, sixtiesh, with long hair in braids like that of many Indians of the district, wore a red shirt, with a long, black bow tie, and green pants tucked into high, yellow Spanish-type boots. Two big, long-barreled Colt revolvers hung from a wide leather belt. Very dashing and colorful indeed was this colonel!

"Come in! Come in, *mi general*, my home is your home. Make yourself and your gringo friend comfortable. I will have dinner served at once, as you are probably very hungry after your long ride."

The general replied, "*Muchas gracias, mi coronel*, yes, we are very hungry. My partner and I can surely eat, as we have traveled far today. Outside we have eight *peones* and mules with our equipment for prospecting. We have come to inspect your gold mine, if that is your wish."

The colonel smiled at us and said, "Fine! I am most happy that you have come. I will send a *mozo* to take care of your beasts and to see that your men are fed and given a place to sleep." Soon we were sitting at a big table and were being served by a boy and two pretty young girls. It was some of the finest food I have ever eaten.

"Well," said the general at last, "we have had quite a ride today. As we came through the village, we noticed that some men had been fighting with guns. In the cantina were three dead men lying on the floor."

The colonel began, "It was like this, *mi general*——."

The general started to laugh, "I knew it! I knew that it had to be you."

Then the colonel continued, "You see, *mi general*, that is

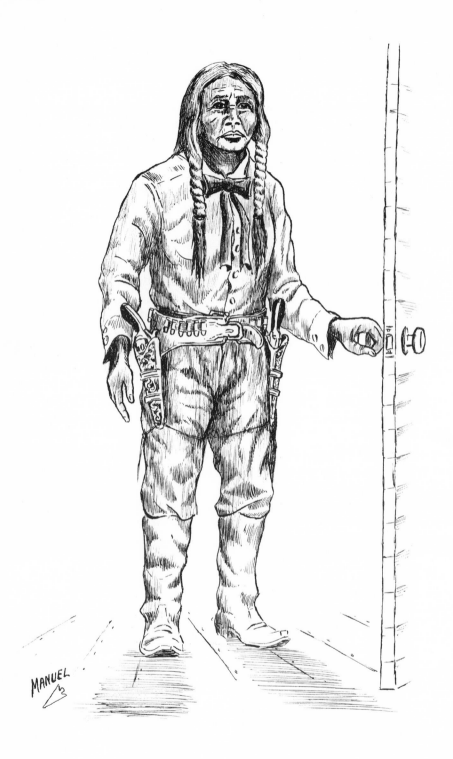

my cantina. Today I went to check with the *cantinero* and to make out orders. When I was behind the bar counting the money, one of these men came back where I was working and said to me, '*Coronel*, they say that you are not a man, but that you are really a woman. I am going to take off your pants and find out the truth.' I told him to get out, but he drew a long knife and came at me, so I shot him. His friends then drew their guns and started to shoot at me, so I jumped up on the bar and shot everyone that had a gun in his hand. Two of the men ran; the other three are there in the cantina."

"Yes," said the general. "Very good shooting, *mi coronel*, and you had good luck not to catch a bullet with so many shooting at you. Those men who ran did not go far. They are both a short way down the street, quite dead. You are as good with your *pistolas* as you were during the revolution!" The general laughed long and loud.

It has always been hard for me to understand how Mexicans can hold human life so cheaply, and consider the death of a man—five men—by violence to be some kind of grisly joke. Strange as it may be, they seem to hold their own lives as cheaply.

Then, as though having dead men all around were the normal course of everyday living, the general said, "Please pass me some more of that fine beef, *mi coronel*. That is the best beef I have eaten since we were fighting together in the revolution and eating the best we could steal." Again his big booming laugh rang out.

The two old soldiers talked of their experiences and of old friends until late that night. I much regretted my poor understanding of Spanish, for although I could follow the gist of their tales of the great revolution, had my command of their tongue been better, any one of their experiences would have made an interesting story. At last we were shown our sleeping rooms for the night, which passed peacefully.

The following morning we were all up early and went to the mine, the colonel in the lead, our pack outfit and Indians following with several of the colonel's vaqueros and an enormous amount of food. There was no road; only a horse and mule trail. Those who had worked the mines many lifetimes previously had packed in all their supplies on the backs of mules and burros, and the gold that was recovered was packed out the same way. If the mine were to be worked by modern methods, it would be quite an engineering feat just to bring in the heavy equipment required.

The site was pleasantly situated above a small river, with good feed for the animals. Nothing remained of any buildings except a few stone walls in ruins. Near the river, below the workings, stood two very old *arrastres* to which the ore apparently had been packed. Examination of the old workings, which had stood the years well since the property was abandoned, showed the ore to be rich quartz with much visible gold. Ore such as this is picture rock wherever gold is mined, and would require careful guard against high-grading. Mexican miners are some of the most notorious high-graders known, although every mining district where the ore is rich develops people proficient in this form of thievery. Below the old mine workings, we found some rich placer along the river. The gold probably was derived largely from erosion of the outcropping veins that had been worked. I believed then, and still believe, that this mine could be worked quite profitably by modern methods.

During the ten days we spent exploring the mine and the surrounding area, we found another very old *arrastre* and some caved-in workings farther around the small mountain. This prospect did not appear to be as rich as the first.

We lived well during this time. The colonel had returned to the rancho the second day and had big lunches of fine beef sent out to us each day. When the sampling and exploration was finished we went back down to the rancho to see the colonel, whom I told of our findings, recommending that a competent engineer be hired to get the mine in operation. Both the general and I were convinced that it could be made to pay well if worked properly. The colonel, however, was not interested in working it, but had wanted (his, her) greatly admired old commander to have it, for he had lost much of his wealth in several ill-fated revolutions. We could do as we pleased with it: work it, sell it, or lease it to a large company. The colonel was in the cattle business and had about all one person could handle, fighting cattle thieves and trying to keep order in this little principality; it would be good to have strong friends down at that end of the rancho to keep the cattle thieves under control.

After the general had borrowed a thousand pesos from his old colonel, we went on our way. As we rode off, the general said to me, "Always treat her as a man and you will get along very well with the colonel. She does not like people to know that she is a woman, so I always address her as a man. She likes me very much for that, and we have great respect for each other. Be very careful not to make her angry if you come here again, for she shoots first and talks afterward, and is like lightning with those two big guns. You have seen what she can do with them, and she never goes unarmed. I do not believe that she would shoot you, for you are my friend, but always remember that she is dangerous. Perhaps she is only a loco old woman, but do not forget the demonstration of her work you saw as we rode into town."

Nothing could have forced me to do anything to arouse her anger, I told him, and I would hesitate to come back alone. I much preferred the old general's protection when dealing with his trigger-happy friends.

Although we often talked of going back with our miners to open up the mine, too many other things required our attention. Then the general died of his old wounds and mescal, and I was away from Mexico for a long time. I have often thought about this rich little mine, which could make a few men quite wealthy. I do not know if the colonel is still alive but, under the new mining laws, it would be possible to get a concession to work it, whoever owns the rancho. Some day, perhaps, I will go to the good little gold mine of the *coronela* and have it for myself, now that the old general is dead and the politicos have taken nearly everything we once owned.

9

Jungle Gold

MANY YEARS AGO, I was having breakfast with the old general. *Palomas* [doves] were calling in the brush as we ate, and our *mozos* were saddling the horses and mules, preparing for the day's ride. We had stopped for the night at an abandoned hacienda on our way to look over some long-forgotten Spanish mine workings high in the Sierra Madre del Sur.

The general said to me, "*Mi capitán*, I have in my mind a very fine plan. It is even better than robbing trains, which is much fun also, besides being very profitable." In his day he not only had robbed trains, but also had stolen them—and even complete railroads, too; so he knew what he was talking about. "I have long wanted to do this thing which could make many men rich," he continued, "but never until now have I had the right men around me. If we work it right, we will be rich for life. If we make a mistake, we will be cut into small chunks and fed to some wild Indian's pigs."

I asked him what wild idea he had on his mind now, but he said only that he would tell me more as we rode, for we had far to go and should be getting mounted.

We went out and inspected the animals and their packs and lined them out for the day's travel. Soon we were mounted and riding at the head of our long column of men and animals. The general reined up beside me and said, "Here is the story as it was told me by my grandfather, who was not a man to make jokes or idle talk. He surely would have been president of the republic, had he not had the misfortune of getting shot between the eyes. Before he got himself shot, however, he told me about this place. Now I will tell you. Then we will think very hard and plan well. With the help of an old friend, who is also a general, I think we may have a good chance to win one of the richest mines in all the republic.

"In a valley, high in the mountains of Chiapas, there is a big church which was built by a 'black priest.' He was called a black priest because of something he had done, or is said to have done, that was against the rules of the church. As you know, the church in Latin America was very powerful and had strict and cruel laws; the poor priest was excommunicated. He was a good man, however, and went among the wild and fierce Indians where no other priests had the courage to go and tried to Christianize them. He traveled safely through the high mountains until he finally came to this place in Chiapas, where he built a large stone church. He had found a rich vein of gold. Knowing the hunger of the church for gold, he hoped that he might regain its good graces if he could satisfy the appetite of its prelates for the yellow metal. The black priest built his church over this vein and mined it with his Indians, from within the church. This went on for many years. Few people even knew what had become of him.

"At last he became a very old man. One day he told his Indians that it was time for him to go back to his home in Spain. He told them to take good care of the church he had built for them, and another priest like himself, who would love and care for his children, would be sent. He told them that he would send something by the new priest by which they would know that he was the right one and warned them to beware of anyone, priest or not, who might steal the gold or make them slaves. His last words to his sorrowful Indians was that they should always guard their fine church against strangers.

"The old priest never returned, nor did another priest come to take his place. As the years passed, the church in the jungle was forgotten. It was far from any road, and in high jungle country where few civilized men had ever traveled. The Indians soon forgot much of what the old priest had taught them, and their *brujos* [witch doctors] eventually developed a cult or religion based partly on such Christian teachings as they remembered from the old priest, but mostly on their old pagan beliefs and superstitions. The mine was kept hidden, and no outsider was permitted to go into the church. They believed that terrible disasters would come to them if anyone except the right priest were allowed to work the mine or hold services.

"Several times parties of priests, miners, and others who had heard the legend of the mine in the church tried to get into the valley and find it. The jungle is dense and wild and wet—full of bugs that bite and sting, and *tigres* [jaguars] and fevers. The valley also is guarded well by the wild Indians who shoot with arrows from hiding—you never know when you may be ambushed. All the attempts to get to the mine and hold it have failed, and the church with its rich gold mine now is only a misty legend, known to but few men. Of these, I am sure that I am the only one who has enough information to be able to find it."

I had listened spellbound to his long recital. It set my blood racing, for the old general was a man who could speak well in three languages—no illiterate Indian, this one. I knew that he completely believed all he had told me, for it was easy to see that he was eager to start on the search. Like most Mexican generals of Spanish blood, he was a shrewd man, and dearly loved a peso. Unless he was sure that a venture had a strong chance of turning out profitably, he would not risk his money or his hide.

"How are you sure that you can find this place?" I asked. "The jungle of Chiapas is not a good place for white men. Chiapas is a very big state and much of it is unknown to any white man, and to few Indians. I have prospected in parts of Chiapas, and it is hard to find your way around, once you leave the villages. In many places there are no roads and only a few Indian trails. The lowlands are unhealthy and unpleasant, and the Indians can be hostile. Unless a man has a good map and is strong and healthy, he might walk into the jungle and never come out, and his body would never be found."

He smiled and said, "My grandfather had a map given him by a priest who was his friend. This priest had gone into this terrible place with one of the parties of *religiosos*. There were no miners in this large, well-equipped party, and he was the only one to return. All his companions were brutally massacred and chopped up by this fierce tribe of *indios*. This priest got out with only his life, the map, and one piece of ore, which was rich, rotten quartz with more gold than gangue. My grandfather showed it to me years ago, and I still remember how the gold looked—as though it was just holding the quartz crystals together.

"The priest had told him that the mine was beneath the church, and that one must go behind the altar and down some stone steps into a kind of vault with a stone door. Behind this door are the mine workings. They are not extensive, only a shaft, but this shaft was sunk on a vein of the very rich, rotten quartz, all like the sample given my grandfather, which had nearly cost the priest his life.

"My grandfather liked mines, but he was busy fighting the French, then other generals and their armies, and he had his big ranches and good mines in the north that kept him busy. He never did get around to going up into those mountains in Chiapas to find this mine in the church. I now have the map among my many papers that came to me from our old home. That is why I believe that, if we plan well, we may be able to find this mine and have it for ourselves."

Now the grandson of one of the old national heroes was telling me of these events of so long ago, as we rode along a high trail. With his map, we might stand a good chance of replenishing our fortunes quickly. Such things have happened in Mexico, and the possibility is never far from the minds of those who follow the lure of gold in the world's lonely places.

"*Mi general*," I said, "this will be an expensive undertaking. It is seldom possible to rent mules in the wild country of Chiapas. We would have to plan on buying them, and the cost of supplies and our transportation from Mexico will be considerable. Will we be able to finance such an expensive trip?" During this time we were having many reverses and had been forced to pass up potentially profitable ventures for lack of capital.

"Do not worry, my boy. I have just told you that the estate of my family in the north has been settled; the map is not the only thing of value I have received. Although I am not as rich as I once was, I shall not have to worry about expenses for anything I might like to do for a long time. I will pay all the expenses, for without you and my old friend, whom I trust like a brother, the map that will lead us to this rich mine could not be used. When we have the gold, I will recover the expenses, for I surely believe the mine will be ours."

This statement brightened things considerably for me, and I said that under such circumstances I would be most happy to be included in the venture. "But," I asked, "how do you intend to gain the trust of the Indians so they will allow us to get to the mine? How may we expect to be successful where so many have failed in the past?"

The general said that he had been giving this much thought and, when he told me his plan, it was not hard to see how he had become a general at an age when most officers of his class were still majors. "This friend of mine, who has been mostly in the north, studied for the priesthood when he was young," he said. "He did not take holy orders, because he fell in love and married. He became a soldier, and finally a general. He is tall and thin and does not look like a fat Spanish priest as I do, but he can teach me. I will buy the robes and all the things we will need, and he can teach me how to act like a priest and to use the things of the mass. For him I will buy the clothing of a monk, and you can be the acolyte. We will practice the use of all the things of the church and learn to celebrate the mass. I am sure we will be able to fool these ignorant Indians of the jungle, who probably have never seen a white man, and surely not a priest. This is the best plan that I have been able to think of, and the only one that would have any chance of success. We could, of course, let the government know about the mine and get troops to take it. But I have no desire to let some big politico in the capital have our mine, and that might happen if we have government troops, and if people who do not like me very much were to know about it."

On our return to Mexico City the general bought the robes

and all the other ecclesiastical items that would be needed, under the direction of the other general. We then spent many days in practicing to act like dedicated churchmen until we could go through a mass and felt comfortable in our new clothing. It was hardest for us to learn to talk properly, for we were all rough *campesinos* and soldiers in our talk. Anything else would have been resented by our miners and *arrieros* [mule drivers] and to talk like a *gachupín* [Spaniard] when in the *campo* often is an invitation for a long, sharp knife when one's back is turned. The revolution still lives.

The general, who knew some Latin, soon was giving a fine imitation of a well-fed and properly instructed Spanish priest. The other general, having gone through most of the schooling for the priesthood, had no trouble in filling his part convincingly. Fortunately, it would not be necessary for me to do any talking. As long as I was able to go through the proper motions and learn where to stand and what to get for the priest during the mass, I did not believe that the simple Indians in the back country would see through my disguise.

At last the general felt that we were ready for a test. He asked his wife for her opinion. Having been gently raised by the nuns before the revolution, she had proper respect for the church and did not approve of what we were doing. She said to the general, "You are big enough and fat enough and a big enough thief. Maybe you are smart enough too, but those Indians also are smart. I am very glad that I am not going with you!"

The general threw up his hands, turned to us, and said, "See, you can never please a woman; I get no thanks. When I lost the revolution, she gave me hell. When I lost the big house in Coyoacán she said that it was my fault and, when we had to leave the republic and go to France and the United States so that my enemies in the new government would not have me shot, she had no sympathy." We knew that he was joking, for rough and ruthless as he may have been, he loved his wife as he loved nothing or no one else.

He continued, "Now she laughs at me because I am trying to get a rich mine, and in the only way that I know how without killing many people, or being killed ourselves. Well, I believe in doing things the best way that I can, so now that we have worked at making a mass and I have learned to act like a priest, we should go to some small town where there is no priest and try out our work on some Indians. It is the Indians who must be pleased, not my wife. If we can fool the smart Indians of the town, then we should have no great trouble with the wild Indians in the jungle. I must keep away from real priests, for a real priest could tell the difference. It might be hard to explain why we are dressed like this. I know a place that will be right for our purpose."

We all got into the general's old Packard and started for the small town about fifty miles from the capital. I drove and the two generals, in their clerical robes, sat in the back seat. They really looked the part they were playing and, had I not known them so well, I wouldn't have suspected that they were anything else.

We arrived at the little pueblo and parked in the plaza. The general got out and walked beneath the big eucalyptus trees, and some Indians came up to him. The poor Indians knelt and kissed his hand, and soon many more came to be blessed. Both generals had their hands full, giving each Indian their blessing. Many wanted the "priest" to hear their confessions. A large number brought gifts. One came running with a turkey, and another brought a live pig, others brought eggs, fruit, hot tortillas and enchiladas, and a big sack of beans. I loaded the old Packard with all of this loot while the generals said their goodbyes and promised they would try to come again.

As we left these kind and trusting people, I could see that

the general was very much upset, and he said, "I certainly hated to fool those good and pious people; this is the worst thing that I have ever done in my life. Look at all the fruit and those chickens and animals they have given us. I am ashamed of myself for taking all these things, which they need for themselves; but I am a miner at heart, and my family has been miners for centuries; so goddammit, I am going to have this gold mine yet! If we could fool those smart town Indians, I surely can handle the wild ones in the mountains of Chiapas, who don't even know how a priest should act. Then, too, these things will be fine eating. It is no wonder that priests are fat. Although I am ashamed of myself, I am also glad, because it worked. We shall leave at once for Chiapas while our luck is working so good."

A few days later we were climbing off the train at Teapa, on the Tabasco-Chiapas line. The short train with its little engine moved out of the station and chugged on her way to Campeche, leaving us there in the afternoon rain. Having dressed in rough clothes, we had the altar things, candles, and vestments stored safely in our bags. We bought mules and rode southeast to the Río Tacotalpa. The river winds back up into country where there are no roads and, if you cross the divide and follow the streams on the other side far enough, they will take you into Guatemala. This country has never been thoroughly explored, and thousands of square miles probably have never been walked over by a white man. There are some mountain ranges in there that are very rough and some volcanic peaks that appear to be very high, many of which still show a plume of smoke.

We were north and east of these mountains. Our map showed that we should turn away from the river we were finally following about forty miles from the Guatemala border and head northeast. This country is still plenty wild; even now, it is almost as it was when Cortés first came to Mexico.

The rainy season is long and heavy and there is always rain
in the afternoon, even in the dry season. The climate is hot
and close, like the interior of Panama. The mosquitos, so thick
in some places that when you wipe your face you get a hand-
ful of blood, cause malaria so virulent as to make a man fall
in his tracks. There are guinea worms that get into your skin
and stay for a year before you can get rid of them; they give
you pure hell. There is also a fly that injects its eggs under
your skin; the bugs then hatch in a little silk sac, causing
great pain and perhaps serious infection. But there are lots of
minerals in this terrible country, even more in Guatemala
than in Chiapas.

When we could find a place with fewer mosquitos and
other pests, we would make our overnight camp, but the roar
of the many kinds of frogs and night-ranging animals, added
to the stinging and itching caused by the countless insects,
made sleep nearly impossible. The generals, both well past
middle age and carrying lead from old battles, sat their mules
like young boys and never complained. They didn't even slap
at the mosquitos, which were nearly driving me mad. These
men were of a special breed, descendants of the conquistado-
res; no longer does Mother Mexico breed such as these. All
this difficult travel and the many hardships would have
turned lesser men back to their easy life, but not my generals.
They just took whatever the day gave and never whimpered.
They were *muy hombre* [real men]. Only once did the old
general say, "*Capitán*, be sure and keep our robes dry and
clean if you can."

After two and a half days of this terrible jungle travel, we
began to get into higher country, where the heat did not sap
our strength as badly and where there were fewer mosquitos
and stinging bugs. We came at last to a thick forest of big
hardwood trees, with a few mahogany trees among them—
quite valuable, if there were a way to harvest them and get

them to a buyer. In this place there were many grasshoppers about four inches long, and flying lizards that climbed into trees and glided from the height, like flying squirrels. Often they would glide all the way to the ground and fold their wings; then they must crawl or climb like any other reptile. We had many fine meals of grasshoppers mixed with dried eggs and chiles—which we had brought with us—a tasty meal, much better than it sounds.

We made camp on the edge of these dense woods, for we were sure that we were not far from the Indians and the valley with its church and mine. We planned to rest here while preparing to meet these people. The generals, putting on their robes, looked fine.

That night we heard the big cats scream. These were *tigre*, or jaguar, and they grow to enormous size in this area. I have seen some whose heads looked as big as a bushel basket and probably would measure nearly ten feet from nose to end of tail. These are real American leopards and can be quite dangerous. Many Indians have lost their lives to these great cats and, unless well armed, a man had better avoid them. Whenever the *tigre* screamed, our mules tried to get into bed with us. They would kneel down on their forelegs and try to nose their way into our serapes. Mexican mules know that the big cats have a fondness for mule meat.

Giant fireflies were thick at the edge of the timber, and soon we saw a brighter light far off in the woods. I was too tired and insect-bitten to wonder about it. I just rolled up in my serape, covered my head, and went to sleep. The generals stayed awake longer to watch the light. As I fell asleep, they were still speculating on it. In the morning they told me that it was a torch carried by some Indians fire fishing. They had passed a short distance from our camp, then gone on up the small stream without seeing us.

The following morning we started up the stream. The trail

was bad, and we had to walk and lead the mules. Soon the stream entered a deep cañon with high, nearly perpendicular, walls. There were enormous boulders on the cañon floor, and we had not gone far until the mules no longer could pass between them. We stopped to make coffee and to decide on our next move.

Finally the general said, "Here we must leave the mules. We will have to hobble them and hope that they do not get killed by the *tigre* before we can get back. I think we should wait here until some Indians pass by; we should let them come to us. Perhaps we can become friendly with some of them, and they will guide us to their valley. That would be better than going to their village without their knowing that we are peaceful. I, for one, do not want to have any of those long arrows shot at me. There are bird traps here and this is a well-used trail; some Indians will be coming by this place before the day is over."

Hardly an hour had passed when five Indians in big straw hats came down the trail. They had long hair and strings of animal teeth and dried bugs around their necks, and were wearing nothing but little skirts around their waists. When they saw us, they stopped and stared. The old general, in his brown robes, with a golden rope around his waist, gold rimmed eyeglasses, and cork helmet, looked like a real priest. Taking his beads in one hand and his big silver cross in the other, he walked toward the Indians. Three ran away, but one old man and another Indian stood their ground. The general walked right up to them, talking all the time in Spanish.

It certainly looked like the end of the old general. The younger Indian fitted an arrow to his big bow. He did not draw it, however, and the general kept on talking.

Finally the old Indian knelt down and kissed the general's hand and said in very poor Spanish, "Pardon me, Father. It has been long since I have heard the tongue of my Father, or spoken it. I am the only one of these people who speaks Spanish. We live half a day's travel from here. Only a few of the older people have seen a white man. You are the only ones to come to our land for many years. I am their *brujo* [witch doctor, medicine man, shaman] and the old chief and I are leaders of our people. The chief is very old and I keep him alive with my herbs and medicine. When I am no longer able to keep the old chief alive with my magic, this young man will become our chief, for he is the son of the old chief and is a powerful warrior."[4]

The general told the old man that he had come from Spain, for he knew that, although they had a church, they had not had a priest for many years. "We have come from far away, across the big water, to help your people and to take care of your church," he told them. "Many years ago, my people sent you the priest who built your church. Many wars have kept them from sending another until now. We are sorry that you have been so long without a priest, as your first priest promised to send another. Now we are here after many moons of dangerous travel over the big water, through the jungle, and into these mountains. Take us to your people and to the church, for we must work to get it ready for your first mass."

The *brujo* told the big Indian with the bow what he had said, and the other general brought a can of sardines and a

[4] The expedition appears to have penetrated the Lacandón Forest of the Eastern Highlands of Chiapas, and the Indians probably were a remnant of the Chol, of Mayan origin (Cholan linguistic group), who originally inhabited the area. In 1564 Fray Pedro Lorenzo undertook this group's conversion and move to the northern extremity of Chiapas, adjacent to the Tabasco border, where they reside today. Despite their early contact with missionaries, the Chol clung stubbornly to their ancient way of life. It is interesting to note that El Lobo thought he recognized the language of the Indians this party met as a Mayan dialect. Their dwellings were wattle and thatch, similar to those of the Mayas in other areas.

drink of mescal for everyone. The Indians drank the mescal, and the big buck lay down his bow and sat with the rest of us while we ate the sardines. But they did not ask us to come with them to their village.

The general repeated what he had said. The quicker we got the church fixed up, the quicker we could hold services in it. Of course what the general really wanted was to get at the gold mine beneath the church, but we knew that only the most careful diplomacy would allow us to live, to say nothing of gaining possession of the mine. After much more talk and a present of several cans of sardines, the *brujo* said we could go with them to their village and talk with the chief; only the chief could make a final decision.

It was easy to see that these two did not like us very much. The *brujo* probably thought a priest would reduce his power over the other Indians, and the young Indian likely was thinking he himself would be a big man among his people if he killed a white man. We all feared they would try to kill us when they had help. I have had contact with the more primitive Indians in many parts of Latin America, and few have ever given me so much reason to be afraid.

The *brujo* told us that horses and mules could not get up to the village on the trail we were on. He promised to send some boys to bring the animals and our gear to the village on the longer trail. We would continue up the cañon, as this path would allow us to reach the village before dark. The Indians led the way.

The generals held their robes up out of the water as we crossed and recrossed the little stream. They were hard put to keep from tripping in the unaccustomed apparel. They were beginning to show the strain of the arduous trip, and old wounds brought involuntary groans from their clenched teeth. The old general from the north carried a heavy bullet in his hip, which made such hard walking very painful, but he just held a grim expression and pushed on up the cañon. The other, I knew, had been shot many times, for I had seen him stripped when we had bathed in mountain streams. He had sabre cuts and battle scars all over his body, and once a field piece had blown up beside him, killing all those around him. He still carried several bullets in his body.

I joked with him and told him he should work hard at being a priest, because he was too old and shot up to be a good general any more. He should let people kiss his hand, then talk them out of their pigs and chickens, for he could never lead a revolution again. He cursed me in French and English and said that he would have me executed as soon as we got out of the predicament we were in. The *brujo* asked what language we were speaking, and the general told him we spoke the language of priests, but I don't think the old Indian believed him.

At last the path ran into the cañon wall, and we climbed straight up it on ladders made of hardwood logs, notched and lashed together with lianas. The steps were deeply worn, for the Indians carried their village's sustenance up the crude ladders from the cañon. There were natural terraces in the cliff wall, many with deep soil and growing crops. Above us, as we climbed toward the village, groups of Indians were clearing rocks from other terraces for new corn land. Tons of large and small rocks came hurtling down the cañon, bouncing about as they crashed to the bottom. When we approached these places, the *brujo* would yell up to the workers, and an answer would come floating back. Then we would climb again while they waited for us to get up to their level. I liked the looks of neither these Indians nor the surroundings.

After hours of climbing, we came to a branch in the cañon,

MANUEL

nearly at the top. Here we found an old mine dump, unbelievable as it may seem in this god-forgotten place that looked as though no white man had ever set foot there before.

The cañon was so deep and the rocks walls so nearly perpendicular that the sun struck the floor for no more than a few minutes a day. The old dump ran along one wall of this branch cañon. Much of it probably had been washed away by the torrents that rush down the mountain cañons during the rainy season, but about an acre was left, held by the enormous boulders on the cañon floor. Ruins of several stone houses could be seen, built close to the cañon wall. A mine tunnel had been driven into the wall near the houses, and a small stream flowed from it.

The old general said, "Don't even look at it, for I don't want this damned *brujo* to know that we have any interest in mines." I told them that I had a stone in my boot and sat down to take it off while the others climbed slowly upward. As soon as I was sure I was not being watched, I picked up a few pieces of rock from the dump. It was high-grade silver-lead ore, and there were many pieces larger than a man's head without any gangue. In a less remote area this would have been a valuable mine.

At last we reached the top and looked over the high ridge into a deep, closed valley, perhaps an ancient crater. Mist and smoke lay over the little basin, and here and there were small clearings where the Indians were preparing the land for planting corn. This place had a bad look to it and, with what I had seen of the Indians so far, I must admit that I was beginning to be afraid. The village could not be seen because of the smoke and large trees that grew everywhere except on the land that had been cleared for the *milpas* [fields].

The village lay in the center of the valley. Suddenly the chief's son left us, running; the *brujo* said that he was going to get horses for us. Soon a couple of youngsters showed up with two horses, so the generals rode and I walked with the *brujo*. We arrived at the village just as darkness was falling. The old general went with the *brujo* to talk with the chief while the other general and I lay down in the little hut they provided. A big crowd of women and children of all ages came to look us over. Most apparently had never seen a white man. We were quite the center of attraction. The young girls pointed and talked about us to each other, and the children chattered and touched our clothes, for they never had seen such a sight. One very old woman who spoke a little Spanish had been carried by the others to see us. Telling us that she was the daughter of one of the former chiefs, she urged us to leave the valley at once, as it was a dangerous place; her people, being suspicious of all strangers, killed all who entered their land.

She confirmed my suspicion that we might find ourselves in a bad way before we ever got out of there. I was glad that we had kept our pistols concealed on us, instead of leaving them in the packs on the mules, as we had considered doing. I gave the old woman a cheap silver ring that I had picked up at the *mercado* [market] of a little town hundreds of miles away. It was a small price for her warning, but she valued it highly.

The women wore their hair much longer than the men but, except for the little grass skirts, they wore no clothing. Men and women dressed alike, while the children wore nothing except perhaps a string of dried bugs around the neck. No foot covering of any kind was seen on any of them, but all had widely splayed toes and broad feet with horny soles. The sharp rocks upon which they trod in the course of their daily lives probably caused them little discomfort, for they had lived on them from birth.

Near the hut, where we rested while the old general was having his conference with the chief, was what appeared to be a large igneous intrusion. Whether the dikes that rose above the valley floor had been exposed by erosion or by earthquake could not be determined without careful examinination, which was impossible if we were to conceal our interest in minerals. Nevertheless, I was pricked by curiosity—a strange circumstance when we might feel an arrow at any moment. A short distance from the village, a single church belfry could be seen, rising above the thick trees. So close we now seemed to the end of our quest, yet so far in actuality!

The general finally returned from his visit to the chief. "I had much trouble getting his permission to do anything with the church," he announced. "I do not believe that the *brujo* was much help either; he is liable to make trouble for us, and we must watch him closely. I also believe that the old chief can understand some Spanish, and perhaps some of the others also. We must be careful in our talk and speak English as much as possible. Tomorrow we start cleaning up the old church and will see what we shall find."

At daybreak we were brought fresh meat and pineapples. After we had eaten, we led a procession of Indians to the church, which indeed appeared old. Churches built by the early Spanish priests in America are not like those built later. They have but little decoration, and the domes and arches are different. It was apparent that valley had suffered a violent earthquake at some time since the church was abandoned. One of the twin bell towers had fallen into the central dome. A side wall had been raised by a fault that ran the length of the church and could be traced for a considerable distance beyond.

Even so, the church walls were still standing, as was one of the towers, and most of the roof was in place. Back from the entrance, in semidarkness, stood the great main altar, now piled deep with broken stone and mortar from the fallen tower. Some of the high, narrow windows still held leaded glass

panes, probably brought from Spain in one of the many gal-
leons that had carried vast quantities of gold and silver back
to the motherland. On the walls of this magnificent ruin were
some old paintings and inlays still discernible despite the
earthquakes and centuries of neglect.

Behind the church was a mine dump, but there was no sign
of a shaft or other opening from which the ore might have
come, or evidence that such an opening might have been concealed. To disguise our real interest, we all ignored the dump
as much as we could. According to the old parchment map,
the only opening to the riches was inside the church, behind
and below the altar. Tons of rubble would have to be moved
before we could know if our expectations would be realized.

"Now," I said to the old general, "you are the priest; you
are also the boss and you will probably be the first one they
will shoot. So get your goddam Indians together and we will
see if you are as good a man as the real priest who built this
place, and also whether you will be able to rebuild it. We will
work; you talk, and talk fast. If these Indians are working,
they won't be making plans to kill us."

By this time the *brujo*, the old chief and his son, and many
other Indians had gathered around us. The general, with the
help of the *brujo*, told them what we wanted done. It was a
very impressive talk he gave. I almost started to believe him
myself. I am sure that none of the Indians suspected that he
was anything but what he claimed to be. The general was
talking for our lives and for a rich gold mine, and he really
worked at it. When he was finished, he started to work at
moving the rubble, as did the other general and myself, carrying the fallen rock and mortar and roof timbers from the
church. The Indians started to work too, and by noon we had
made considerable progress.

Going up into the bell tower that was still standing, I found
five big copper or brass bells and another smaller one. They

had fallen from their supports, the rawhide lashings having rotted long ago, but the tropical hardwood beams that had held them seemed as solid as the day they were put there. I reinforced the supports and, with the help of several husky young savages and some prize poles, soon had the bells rehung. The third day of hard work saw the church sufficiently cleaned up for holding mass. I rang the bells long and loud, and this made the wild Indians happy. We thought we were doing fine and that the mines beneath the church soon would be ours.

The rubble removed, we found deeply worn stone steps behind the altar, leading downward. The old priest's miners must have made many trips down into the mine and back, carrying *morrales* [knapsacks] of ore and waste rock suspended from their heads. They were the great and great-great grandfathers of the Indians now cleaning up the old ruin.

The outer walls were more than ten feet from inside surface to outside. Within these walls were passages and stairways. One set of steps led to the belfry, but another, which we did not get cleaned out, led downward. These also were deeply worn and may have been a second entrance to the mine.

The old Spaniards, being good miners, nearly always had more than one entrance to their mines, which usually were well ventilated in their main workings. It was easy to see that this was a highly mineralized zone, for the fault that had raised one side of the church had exposed good ore. I did not dare make much of a study of the geology with these suspicious savages watching our every move.

Clearing the stones and rubble from the steps behind the altar, we came to the great stone door, which had been described to the general's grandfather. It had been cut from a single piece of basalt and must have weighed a ton or more. We dared not attempt to move it, with the Indians all about, but decided to try to win their confidence first. We felt that we were making progress, although the Indians continued sullen and watchful. But then our hopes were dashed.

One night the *brujo* came to our little shack and sat and smoked with us. After a while he spoke. "I have bad news for you. The chief says that you are not a good priest and in the morning you are all to leave. Your mules will be brought to you at daylight, and it is best that you leave at once. As you know, these people know nothing of the power of the white men and are very dangerous. They do not like your coming here and making them work. The chief wants to kill you, but I have told him that if we should do so, many other white men would come to find you and kill many of us if they learned what had happened to you."

The general and I exchanged glances. So close to the gold, and now this had to happen! I asked the general what he thought we should do. Did we dare defy them with only our handguns?

He replied in English, "Just show me a trail out of here and give me my mule. I'll leave this place *muy pronto*. I believe that we are in a dangerous situation and very badly outnumbered." Then he turned to the *brujo*. "We will be ready to leave in the morning if that is the wish of your people. We are unhappy that we cannot stay with our good friends and continue to work on the church and hold masses for them, but we do not wish to make trouble. We will go."

The following morning our mules were waiting; we lost no time in loading the packs and saddling. We told the Indians who had come to see us off that we were sorry to have to leave them, but they would always be our friends, and that we held no anger or enmity toward them. Then, once we were out of their sight, we lost no time in putting into action the time-honored military maneuver of getting the hell out of there.

Afraid they might change their minds and decide to wipe

us out, we rode with hands under our garments, clutching our
pistols. All day we traveled, without a noon stop, pressed by
that eerie feeling of expectancy and the dread of an arrow in
the back from a hidden enemy.

Never have I been more frightened, before or since. The
generals had little beads of sweat on their brows. It is one
thing to know that an enemy is in front of you and that you
will have a fighting chance for survival, but quite another to
ride out of such a savage place knowing that one wrong move
means instant death. To have whipped the mules into a run to
get away would have brought the Indians to a killing frenzy.
In dealing with them, fear was its own worst enemy.

As we rode, we discussed the possibility of our eventual return. Three men alone, we agreed, would never make it; only
a well-armed party prepared to fight it out would have a
chance. The old general, out of favor though he was, thought
that he might be able to persuade the secretary of war that
this country was valuable enough to be opened up for development with the use of troops. There was good land between
the low jungle and the higher mountains that would support
many people if a road were built, and much valuable timber
could be harvested. But such development would take years,
for in Mexico these matters move slowly. Perhaps he could
make the secretary a partner in the mine as an inducement
for him to lend troops for subjecting these savage people.

Our first concern, however, was getting out. Arriving late
that afternoon at the place we first had met the Indians, we
moved on to camp again where we had seen them fire fishing.
Although we had seen no one, we knew that any number of
Indians could have followed us quite unseen. We spent a
watchful night. In the days that followed we continued on
through the jungle and eventually found ourselves back at
Teapa. After selling the mules and gear, we boarded the train

for the capital, subdued but angry over the results of our well-planned but futile efforts.

The general died of his old wounds and too much tequila before our plans to return could be effected. The other general had neither the influence nor the spark of genius that my old general had; no other attempt has been made to get to the mine under the church.

Have I any plans? Not really, for although I have friends who might be able to get official aid, I do not believe that anything short of a small war could open that area to white men. Those wild Indians are living a good life—probably better than if civilization were forced on them. I no longer have the zest for conquest that we knew when the old general, with his wild plans, was alive.

El Lobo and I, in the cantina of a little mountain pueblo, in the late 1940's, ate and drank of the best the place afforded, for today we were muy rico. *We had come out of the mountains in our ragged clothes and worn-out boots, but in the alforjas of our mules had been a small fortune. Now we were clean from hot baths at the small hotel and were dressed in the finest clothing Don Jorge's* ropería *could furnish. We were quietly celebrating the fortuity of our having completed this prospecting trip so profitably, and having come out of the jungle alive.*

Too often, the profit was lacking, and we had to enter the towns circumspectly, lest those to whom we owed money find us before we again had melted into the mountains or the jungle. Tonight we owed no man—not in this town, at least. We had much to be happy for. Perhaps we would grow very expansive before we again faded into the bush and would throw a gran baile *[big dance] and invite all the town.*

My companion, feeling the effects of food and drink, wanted to talk. We discussed our wild experiences in many places, and he asked if he had ever told me of the mines in the Sierra Madre del Sur above the town of Chichihualco, off the beaten track in the State of Guerrero. I replied that he had not, and he began to relate his adventure of perhaps ten years earlier.

10

The Gringo Miner

For a long time I worked for the old general when he was powerful and held a high office in the national government in Mexico. He had many old maps and papers telling of mines lost or hidden by the Spaniards when they were about to be driven from Mexico. I was born with the curse on me to hunt for lost mines and buried treasure, and the general and I got along very well. Sometimes we found valuable treasures that his old *derroteros* [charts] had led us to.

One day, when I had just returned from a trip in rags, about dead from sleeping on the ground and living among half-wild Indians, he said to me, "My boy, have a drink, then go to my home and get a bath and change into clean clothes, and come to my office. I believe that I have something very good in hand for us, and now is the time to act."

After I had cleaned up and drunk some more of the general's fine brandy—his home was as my own and a room was always ready for me—I returned to his office in the *palacio*. He had instructed his secretary and, as soon as he was free, I went in ahead of the many people waiting to see him, among them some high military officers.

"In the pueblo of Chichihualco, Guerrero, about thirty-five kilometers west of the main road, there is the home of an Indian who was a friend of mine during the great revolution. This Indian has told me of some mines, high on the side of a mountain near the town. One of these mines, he tells me, is named El Conde, another is La Condesa, and the third is Los Tres Muertos; not far from these mines is another called Cruz de Fierro [The Count, The Countess, Three Dead Men, and Iron Cross].

"I have reason to believe that these may be good mines and perhaps we could sell them to the big gringo mining company that has written asking me to find them some properties. The timber up there on the mountain is thick and the brush deep, and it is hard to find these mines. It is so long since they have been worked that the dumps have big trees on them, my Indian tells me. You will go to this Indian, Juan Pérez, and tell him that you are the man I told him I would send. I have warned him that, if anything should happen to the gringo that I send, I will kill him and also anyone else I find up there in those mountains. Do not worry about the bandits bothering you, my boy; if they kill you I will take some troops and give them hell."

When I pointed out to him that it would do no good to go in there with troops after I was dead, he told me that there was a detachment of soldiers already in that area, hunting cattle thieves and bandits, but I should have no trouble unless I went looking for it. "Just sample the dumps and workings, and when you get back we will have them assayed. If there is

enough gold and silver, I will condemn them and sell them to
this big company. The Indian Juan believes that some of the
old workings may have gas, for no one has been in them for
many years. Be careful, but bring back the samples as soon as
you can."

I had supper with the general that evening, and we had a
few drinks. I went to bed early and got a good night's sleep
in a civilized bed for a change and was on the bus by daylight. I left the bus at Zumpango del Río, which was where
the road to Chichihualco joins the main highway. I found
that no bus went to the other town, and there were neither
horses nor mules to be had. At the *mercado* I bought a ripe
pineapple and some tortillas, frijoles, and dried meat. With
only my serape, sampling pick, and the food, I started off
down the road afoot. That night I slept in an Indian jacal and
the next morning rented a mule from my host.

Traveling was faster on the mule, and that afternoon
found me at the home of the Indian Juan, whom the general
had sent me to find. He was an intelligent man, past middle
age but tough and strong. Planning an early start next morning, we went to bed early. A loud knock at the door waked us
about ten o'clock, and we both went to the door to find several
soldiers, with a sergeant in command, standing there. The
sergeant asked me who I was and what I was doing in the
mountains away from the main roads, where it was not safe
for a gringo to be unless he was an outlaw. I told him that I
was a *gambusino*, looking for some mines.

"There are no mines here," he said. "How do I know you
are not one of the bandits that we are hunting? Show me your
papers."

I gave him the order the general had given me for just such
a purpose. It was all very official and looked important.

The sergeant slowly spelled out the writing, then handed
it back to me. He knew Mexican generals, and knew that, al-

though the general might forgive a disservice to himself, an injury to a friend would get him shot quickly. "Señor," he said, saluting, "I am Sergeant Juan López. I am at your service and I shall do my best to help you and the general. You must move to a better house and I will post a guard to protect you."

I told him that I was doing all right where I was, for we would start on a prospecting trip next morning. But he insisted on leaving a guard and also that we accompany him on a tour of the two cantinas to cement our friendship. While we were at one of the cantinas, he noticed that one of my boots needed fixing and sent a soldier to wake the poor *zapatero* and bring him to us to fix it.

At daylight the sergeant came and invited me to bring my Indian and come to his camp for breakfast. He also brought me a fine army mule, which he said I could use until he had to move out of the district or until I had finished my work. This was quite a help, as we couldn't carry all the camp and prospecting equipment on the scrawny mule I had rented. I bought supplies and what prospecting gear I could find in the pueblo, so that both the Indian and I could work at getting samples and trenching in search of veins that had been covered since the revolution of 1910.

Juan Pérez and I left for the mines by the middle of the morning, following a well-worn trail up the steep mountain that rose above the pretty valley. Soon we turned off the trail and ascended a steep faint path that my Indian said would lead to the mines. This had once been a much-used trail, but few except hunters had used it since the mines were abandoned. On we went, up and up, the trail leading among big trees, with vines hanging from the branches, and orchids of many colors. Parrots and large butterflies flew ahead of us, making the jungle colorful and pleasant. High in many of the trees hung great ant nests, which had a tube of the same material extending to the ground to allow the ants to get back to the nests safely during the rainy season. Parrots make holes in these ant nests in which they lay their eggs and hatch their young. The ants apparently do not bother the parrots, but if a man puts his hand into one of these holes he gets bitten badly.

At last we came to a big clearing on a bench where the walls of a large rock house stood. Here we heated our tortillas and beans and rested from the hard climb. The walls, about a meter thick, had been well made of nicely fitted stone. The roof and woodwork had been burned at some time during the revolution, but the flagstone floor, two large fireplaces, and the walls were still in good condition. The Indian said that this had been the home of a gringo miner who had worked El Conde and La Condesa. The ore had been ground in an *arrastre*, then amalgamated in the patio near the house. We found the *arrastre* and the patio still in fair condition. A large tailings dump ran down the side of the hill below the patio. There had been a well-built acequia from a good spring to the *arrastre* and patio, much of which was still as good as new. The Indians of this area must be very good stone workers, for all was built well.

Higher up the mountain we found the mine portal, in solid rock. This tunnel followed a vein about four feet wide and appeared to have two sets of tracks. About a quarter of a mile back in the mountain it branched in many directions. Juan told me that the gringo, in driving the tunnel in an attempt to find the workings of the lost Tres Muertos Mine, had found veins with enough values to pay for the work.

While we were exploring the tunnel and its many drifts and crosscuts, I made an odd discovery. Far back, at the very end of the main tunnel, near the face, I noticed some scraps of paper, used by rats in making a nest. I picked up some of the larger pieces and examined them by the light of my carbide lamp. Printed in English, they were pages from a book on mining. We dug around the rat's nest and found, buried just below the floor of the tunnel, some rotted cow hides in which several old books had been wrapped with a rusty Colt forty-five six-shooter and twenty American double eagle gold pieces.

From the general I later learned more of the story of the gringo and his mine, as we leaned against the Ritz Bar and drank champagne that I had bought with some of the money I had received from the sale of the gold coins. The old Indian Juan who was with me also told me much, as did other older people in Chichihualco.

The gringo had come to the mountain with a steam drill powered by a small wood-burning boiler. This was the first mechanical drill ever seen in the area, and all marveled at the speed holes were drilled in the rock for the dynamite. The drill could do more with one driller and a helper than ten or twelve men drilling by hand. The heavy equipment and a great quantity of supplies had been packed by mules from the railroad up into the mountains. The gringo had brought some men and, hiring many more at Chichihualco, built the big stone house whose ruins we had seen. As many as two hundred men worked in the mine, in the milling of the ore and building.

This gringo said that he had come from the far north of the United States. With him was a beautiful Spanish woman, who had a map of the Cruz de Fierro mine. Her family had owned the mine in Spanish times, but had hidden it and gone back to Spain during the revolution of Hidalgo. This woman had lived in the pueblo. Once a week she would ride sidesaddle up the mountain to the mine to see how the work was progressing.

The mine of the gringo—they call it that, but probably he was either partner with the Spanish woman or was working for her—had been in operation three or four years when the great revolution of 1910 started. The gringo was *muy hombre* and he brought many rifles and mule loads of ammunition into his camp. He told the people who worked for him, "Revolution or no revolution, we are going to work the mine. We are getting near the old Spanish workings now, and if anyone comes here looking for trouble, we will give it to him."

My old Indian guide, who was a young man then, worked for the gringo. He told me, "One day General Salgado and his army came into Chichihualco. They took the town, shot a lot of people, and made all the men who had not been shot join his army. They made the town their headquarters for a time. The Spanish woman had moved to the mine with all her possessions when it became known that General Salgado was approaching the pueblo.

"The gringo had prepared for trouble, but hoped the revolutionists would not climb the rough mountain trails to his mine. He had a very rough Mexican Army captain with him who trained all of the miners to handle rifles. They had many new Winchester carbines and thousands of rounds of ammunition. The gringo also had made some bombs of black powder, and they had plenty of dynamite and caps for many more. They were well fixed to take care of intruders unless an enemy could bring artillery up the steep trails.

"General Salgado sent about a hundred of his troops up the mountain to take care of the gringo and rob his mine. Only five or six came back unwounded, and many did not come back at all. Those who did come back told General Salgado that it was just plain hell up there on the mountain. There had been little cover for the soldiers, but the gringo and his men were forted behind thick stone walls. They told the general that if he wanted the mine he would have to take more men and go up and take it himself. The general had taken over the best cantina, where he had plenty of food, liquor, and women, and was very pleased with himself. In addition, he had robbed several rich mines and stolen many bars of gold and silver. Now he was being prevented from adding to his wealth by a stubborn gringo and a few *peones* with guns."

A very important person indeed was General Salgado, and he was in no frame of mind to permit a stupid gringo prospector to stop him. He drank up his mescal, called his troops, and went up the mountain to slap this mosquito that had bitten him. The gringo had scouts out, and they reported the approach of the revolutionary army almost as soon as it was well started. At many places where the trail was narrow, and below high cliffs, his men dumped dynamite and black powder bombs on the general's troops. When the bombs were gone, they ran to the big stone house and the mine tunnels. There the miners took positions behind rocks and other fortifications.

The little war lasted a week, but so well prepared and trained was the small defensive force that at last the great general, who had struck fear over three states, had to pull out without the bars of silver and gold and many of the men who had come up the mountain with him. He also had lost many horses and mules and wasted thousands of rounds of ammunition. It is hard to understand why he did not bring up his little mountain guns, unless he was short of ammo. Anyhow, he gave it up as a losing game, sending word to the gringo that he would come back and give no quarter to anyone who resisted.

It was not long after this battle that the general was defeated by *federales* and most of his men were killed. He was executed, and so were all his men who had been captured. During the great revolution they really played for keeps and capture often meant death, either by firing squad or by hanging. The revolutionists were considered traitors, and little mercy was shown by federal commanders.

The gringo had found one of the old Spanish tunnels, and I was told by some of the old people in Chichihualco that at one place he had drilled through many feet of plug in an old drift that had been closed by the Spaniards. The cement that held the plug had been made of human bones, hair, and blood. Flies gathered on it when they brought it out to the dump. It is said the Spaniards used up quite a few Indians this way when they plugged their shafts and tunnels to hide them from their enemies. I have heard tales of such, both in Mexico and in the southwestern United States, but have never seen it myself. So many references to such occurrences must have some basis of truth to persist so stubbornly. That way the Indians who did the work could not talk. They were not needed any longer, and since they were slaves their Spanish masters could do as they wished to them. ¡Los muertos no hablan! [The dead do not talk.]

The gringo thought that he was about to enter the rich workings of the old mine when the revolution started. Everyone thought that the fighting would be over soon and that there would be peace. But the war lasted many years, and the gringo finally gave up trying to operate his mine in such times and left Mexico. The Spanish woman left with him. They never returned, and it is not known whether they took the bullion with them or hid it.

It is my belief that there may be much gold in the old Spanish mine. The gringo worked the small veins and stringers he found during the search for the old workings and did very well on this lower-grade ore that had been ignored by the Spaniards. To me this is definite indication that they were working a richer grade. With slave labor the low grade would have paid handsomely.

A very strange incident occurred while we were on the mountain exploring the old workings. I had gone into the ruins of the big stone house and looked around while my In-

dian Juan was preparing *comida* on our way up. There was
some grass and a few small trees growing between the large
flagstones of the floor, but otherwise all appeared as it must
have when it was abandoned and burned. The ground was
hard and the floor seemed to be in place.

We had camped farther up the mountain, near the portal,
where there was fine pasture and good water for the mules.
This was about half a mile above the stone house and the
arrastre and patio where they had milled their ore. When I
was satisfied that we had all the samples that could be taken
without a crew for underground work, we started back to
Chichihualco, for the general wanted a report on the property
as soon as we could evaluate the samples. We stopped at the
stone house on the way down. I do not know why I went into
the ruins, but I did. I was surprised to find someone had been
there while we were working up on the mountain.

Many of the large stones had been removed from the floor.
In a corner of one of the rooms we found a hole several feet
deep, about the size of a steamer trunk. There were rust scales
in the bottom of the hole and on the dirt pile, as though an
iron chest had been removed from its hiding place of many
years.

I have often wondered why this hole was freshly dug just
at the time I was there. It may have been close timing on
someone's part—or maybe only coincidence. Perhaps the
gringo had returned for gold he had hidden when he was
forced to leave. It may have been treasure hunters who had
found it with a metal detector, but few such people would
know of the place. On our return to the pueblo we inquired if
any strangers had been seen heading for the mountain, but
no one admitted having seen any. I am afraid that I missed
finding some treasure that time, but if it was the gringo, I
could not begrudge his recovery of gold that was rightfully
his.

11

Treasure Cave

I FLEW FOR GENERAL CEDILLO when he was governor of the state of San Luis Potosí, and I was also with him during his revolution in which he lost his life. We had long been friends, and he often told me of his experiences. Had not General Cedillo run short of aviation gasoline and good pilots, we surely would have won this revolution.[5]

[5] General Cedillo, who had been governor of San Luis Potosí in the 1920's and had received some support as a possible successor to President Plutarco Elías Calles in 1928, was appointed minister of agriculture by President Lázaro Cárdenas in June, 1935. Resigning in 1938, he became commander of the San Luis Potosí military zone. He resisted politically motivated efforts to transfer him to an area where he had less influence and began plotting his revolution, probably with both Nazi and Communist backing. He proclaimed a crusade to defend re-

Long ago, during the days of the great revolution of 1910, he once told me, he had lost a big battle and had to hide out quickly to save his hide. He and some of his officers had to run to keep from being captured and executed; no one bothered with prisoners. They were afoot, for their horses had given out or had been shot from under them. All were tired, hungry, and sore-footed. They still had their arms and some ammo, and could have put up a pretty good fight against a small patrol, but would have been lost had they run into a large body of enemy troops.

They eventually found themselves in the opal mining area[6] where the general had friends. He decided to hide out here, for who would think to look among a lot of ignorant miners for a revolutionary general and his few remaining officers? One of these friends of the general was an old German who had a good opal mine in which several Mexican miners were employed, a small rancho, and also a little *tienda* [store] where he sold supplies to the local miners, ranchers, and vaqueros. He also bought fine opals and took them in trade at his store. Once or twice a year he would take these fine gems to the coast and ship them to buyers in Germany. The general had done many favors for this man and now went to him for help. Soon the fugitives were opal miners. Before long the wrinkles were gone from their bellies and they had good shoes on their feet.

The mine was far from any regularly traveled road, and several months went by without incident. Since there was no

---

ligion, land, and the sacred rights of property from the "atheistic bolshevistic government." But his revolutionary army failed to materialize. He was caught a few weeks later, in a cave or mine tunnel in the hills, with less than a dozen men, and all were killed.

[6] The opal area was near Pénjamo, Guanajuato. Opals are mined principally in two other locations in Mexico: around Magdalena, Jalisco, and Tequisquiapán, Querétaro.

fighting in that part of the country, they were safe in their disguise. One day a boy on a good horse rode up to the mine to find the German. All stopped work to hear what he had to say.

"My father sent me to find you," he said. "He wishes you to come at once, as something important has happened."

The German, who was a close friend of the boy's father, and the general saddled horses and rode back to the rancho with the boy. When they arrived, they found the boy's father quite excited. One of his cows had failed to come in at milking time the evening before, so he had ridden out to find her trapped in what appeared to be an old mine shaft. The shaft had been covered over with heavy timbers, then with dirt and rocks. Grass had grown on it so that no one could have suspected that it was there. The timbers were old and rotten, and when the cow walked on them, some had broken, and she had fallen part way into the shaft.

This shaft was in a place that showed no signs of mineralization, and the ranchero, who also had been a miner, thought it very strange. Perhaps it had been sunk on a vein that had been mined out and all the material recovered had been carried off to a smelter. He wished the German, the general, and their miners to go with him into the shaft to explore it, for perhaps there was either rich ore or fine opals still to be taken.

The German told his old friend that it was time for him to take his opals to the coast and buy supplies but that he would return soon. They would bring carbide lamps, ropes, and candles, go into the cave, and explore it completely. The old German left for the coast the following day, intending to return in about a week. He was delayed, however, and nearly a month passed.

As soon as he had taken care of his affairs at his home and store, he and the general and several of the general's men prepared their equipment and left for his friend's ranch. They had only gone about half the distance when the ranchero's son approached at a gallop. He handed the German a large gold coin. "My father told me to tell you that he is very ill; he believes that he will die, and you must come to him at once," the boy told him. They rode hard to the rancho and found the old ranchero lying on a *petate* [pallet] on the floor of the *casa*. He appeared to be quite ill and weak, and could talk only in a low voice.

"You did not come," he said, "so I took two of my vaqueros and my sons to the shaft. I entered it with my vaqueros, leaving my sons at the surface to handle the rope when we were ready to come out. We let ourselves down on the rope, and soon came to an incline where we could work our way down without difficulty. Then we came to a black hole. By letting a candle down into it with a *reata* [lariat], we found it to be only a *reata*'s length deep. We went on down to the bottom on ropes and found ourselves in a sort of tunnel. On the floor of this tunnel were the tracks of many horses. The passage had been heavily traveled at some time—like a country road.

"We lighted our candles and followed this road. It led us deep inside the mountain. After walking a kilometer or more, we came to two branch tunnels. We separated to follow different ones from this point, planning to return after five candles had burned down, or sooner if we came to the end of our tunnel. I continued on down the main passage. I never saw my men again.

"Several kilometers—it may have been farther, or perhaps not so far, because it is difficult to judge distance underground —I found an iron door in the tunnel floor. The iron was rotten, and I was able to pry it open. I did not find a great treasure, as I had hoped, but only a black hole. A bad smell came from this hole, and I became afraid. I was sure that there must be gold down there, for there was a heavy timber set across the opening. This timber had deep rope marks, indicating it had been used in hoisting heavy loads. I could see the bottom of the hole by the light of my candle, so I tied my *reata* to the timber and lowered myself into it. I found no gold at the bottom, but another tunnel with tool marks on the sides. Perhaps it was a small natural passage that had been widened. Following it for some distance, I found myself in a big room, almost round and with a high ceiling.

"In this room, which must have been some kind of temple of the Aztecs or some older Indians, there were many carvings and paintings on the walls. No white man had done this work, for it was like what I have seen in ruins that were old before Cortés came to Mexico. In this room were many dead men, some sitting, others lying down, all turned to stone but shrunken like mummies from the ancient tombs. They appeared to be white men and wore a uniform of a kind that I had never seen before. There were many very old guns, some flintlocks and some with a cord that must have served as a fuse to ignite the powder charge. Such things I had never seen. These guns were very rusty and rotten, and the wooden stocks crumbled when I touched them.

"I became very much afraid of all these dead men, as they seemed to be watching me, but I was now even more certain that there must be a great treasure in this place, so well was it guarded by the dead. Many passages led from this room, and I continued my search. The passage I followed led to other rooms. There was black powder on the floor of the cave. I was most careful of my candle near this powder, for I had no desire to die in an explosion in such a place. In some rooms were cannon and cannon balls, saddles, harness, and many other things. At last I came to a small room containing barrels and chests of gold and silver coins. Some of the chests had rotted, like the powder barrels in the other room, spilling coins upon the floor.

"Along one wall were great stacks of black silver bars, very large and too heavy for one man to carry far. Near them was a smaller stack of gold bars. I took the food from my leather *morral* and filled it with gold coins. It was so heavy that I could hardly carry it. My fear had grown, whether from the silence or from being alone in this place of the dead, I do not know. I started to return to the iron door where my *reata* was hanging from the timber, but I became lost. I do not know how long I wandered through the many rooms and passages before I found myself back in the room of the dead men. From there I went to the place of the iron door. By this time I had become ill and had not the strength to climb up the rope with the heavy *morral* full of gold, so I left about half of it and at last was able to climb back to the passage above.

"I was now very sick and had to lie down to regain my strength. When I awoke, I thought that I had rested only about an hour, but it must have been much longer, for my candle had burned out. I lighted another candle, closed the iron door, and followed the tunnel to the place where my two vaqueros had left me to go into the other passages, but the men were not there. The water gourd was where we had left it. I drank some water from the gourd and felt stronger. After waiting several hours, I decided that my vaqueros must have gone to the shaft without waiting for me and by now were probably at the surface, eating with their families. The *cabrones* had left me here, I thought. I swore long at such cowards who would leave their employer and benefactor to die alone in such a place.

"I started back toward the shaft where our long rope had been left hanging, with my sons taking care of it far above in the warm sun. *Gracias á Dios*, it still hung where we had left it. Although weak and ill, I had found much gold and taken enough to buy many things, so I tied the rope to me, and gave it a strong jerk. My sons pulled me up. I saw their faces in the blessed sunshine before I fainted. They lifted me onto my horse and brought me home. When I regained my senses I sent my youngest son to ride fast for my *compadre*. When I asked my other sons what had become of the vaqueros, they told me that no one but I had come out of the shaft, and that I had been in there two days, not just one, as I had thought. I sent men to the hole to be ready to help them get out, but no one else has touched the rope.

"Now I am about to die. You, *compadre*, take this gold and use it to see that my family is never hungry. All the gold in the cave is yours if you wish to take it. There is something very bad in there, for it has made me so sick that I am sure I must die."

The man fainted, and General Cedillo and the German examined and counted the heavy gold coins, all Spanish and very old. When the old rancher was conscious again, the German told him not to worry about his family; they would always eat the same food as did his own. Then he said, "My friend, there is nothing wrong with you that some rest and sun won't cure, for you are still a strong and healthy man." But the old rancher said, "No, I tell you that I must die; please get my vaqueros out of the cave, for they are good men and have families. I am sorry now that I cursed them and left them down in that terrible place."

The wives of the vaqueros still in the cave were much upset at the loss of their men, so General Cedillo went with his own men to the cave, guided by one of the sons of the rancher, leaving the German with the sick man. They went into the cave and searched but did not find them. They found all as the rancher had described—horse tracks on the soft surface of the floor near the shaft, and many passages. They did not, however, find the iron door. None of them became sick, but all efforts to find the men failed. They returned to the surface without incident to learn that the old rancher had died.

After burying the poor man, the general and his men again went into the cave, well equipped and with sufficient food and water for several days' stay. This time they found a few coins and some bars of gold in several places and a number of very old guns in poor condition from rust and rot. The lost vaqueros were not found, and several of the men became ill. They abandoned the search and again returned to the surface. Two of the sick men died, and the others refused to enter the cave again.

These men were brave before an enemy they could see but underground in this eerie cave, which they felt to be haunted by the dead, their courage vanished. They all pledged loyalty to the general—they had fought for him and would do so again—but they would not hunt ghosts and spirits. "If that is your decision," said the general, "to hell with the gold, and those poor devils that are lost down there. They are probably dead anyhow. This is a job for men, not for old women and babies. When I find some real men of courage, I will bring them here and we shall all become wealthy and will no longer have to hide out in the hills, far from the fine food, beautiful women, and music of the capital."

Not long afterward, a large army led by General Carranza swept down from the north. Everyone in the area fled before this great army, which killed and looted as it came. General Cedillo, with the remnants of his staff, went south to Chiapas, where he recruited another army and waited until he could return again to his home in San Luis Potosí. He was restored to favor with the powerful generals who ruled Mexico, got his ranch back, and eventually became governor of San Luis Potosí. He became rich and powerful.

It was during his time as governor that I first met him and became his good friend. While I was at his ranch, where I drilled many water wells, he often spoke to me of the cave and its great hoard of gold. We talked many times of going to it with a well-equipped party and making another attempt to find the gold, which could make us rich for the rest of our lives. Many times the general showed me some of the gold coins the cave had yielded. They were larger and thicker than a silver dollar, about as big as a twenty peso coin, but much thicker and heavier, and were crudely made of very pure gold—probably more than nine hundred fine—and very soft. After General Cedillo had become powerful and had his own army and air force, I bought planes for him and flew them to him from many places. When one has military power in Mexico, he may do many things.

At last the general believed that he had the right men around him, and he made another trip to the cave. He had planned well and had much equipment and food. He was prepared for a long and careful search. This time the two vaqueros were found. One was in a sitting position, propped against the wall of one of the passages that had been missed in the other searches. There were many gold coins beside him, as well as several unburned candles. He must have been overcome by gas and died without attempting to get out. The other vaquero was found in a different passage, lying face down, also with some unused candles and many gold coins and a small gold bar nearby. Both bodies were mummified, with no sign of decomposition except that they were shriveled. The air or gas in the cave must have been responsible.

Only the gold beside the two dead men and several small lots, in other passages, were found. The iron door covering the hole leading to the lower passages, where the old ranchero had found the great store of gold and silver and old weapons, was never discovered.

I made plans to attempt to explore the cave, for the general had told me I could have whatever I found. He had become so powerful by now that the federal government feared him and tried to make him leave San Luis Potosí to become governor of another state, far removed from his powerful army and friends. Not caring to have his teeth pulled, he built up his army and air force, with financial help from many foreigners who hoped for profitable concessions, should he become president. The revolution then started, and we both became too busy to think of exploring the cave.

After the revolution was lost, the general and his staff killed, I had to go far away to escape execution myself, and to stay out of Mexico for many years. It was not until a few years ago that I was safe here again, and there still are many who wish me dead. I have not been able to find the time and money at the same time to attempt to go to the cave and look for the gold. I know how to find the entrance that the general used, and we could go there without any trouble. There is sure to be another hidden entrance, which the old Spaniards entered with their horses. We should be able to get good ventilation and get rid of the gas, or whatever it is that caused the death of the vaqueros and the two men who went into it with the general.

12

Golden Idols

ONCE I KNEW A GRINGO who was in the fine large jail in Toluca. The Mexico and Toluca papers for months carried pictures and articles about him. He had a large factory near Mexico, D.F., in which he made Indian masks and all types of idols and other fake artifacts to sell to the *turistas*. He liked real idols too, and somehow his big *bodega* [warehouse] through the years had become nearly full of them. The generals and myself have given this thing much thought, but we do not understand how such a thing could happen. There is a big politico in the U.S.A., whom you may know or know of, who has a large collection of Mexican idols. The Mexican government has made him return some of these treasures taken from the state of Mexico. There are, however, some bastards who say that the idols he returned are fakes or imitations and that he still has the real ones. I can hardly believe such a terrible accusation, but this is what they say. There are also some very famous people in London who have been asked to return idols and other artifacts of great value to Mexico. I do not understand all this.

Anyone knows that a poor *gambusino* such as myself never goes near old tombs, for they are filled with devils, *muy encantado* [haunted], and have no minerals inside. What prospector would be so foolish as to dig in such places?[7] It is said, and the newspapers claim it is true, that my fine amigo has more than a million dollars U.S. in the Bank of London. He says he has made most of this money from the manufacture of fake idols and other artifacts to sell to *turistas*. The Mexican government, however, says that this is a large lie and that he has made all this money as a *contrabandista*, dealing in authentic idols, which everyone knows belong to the government. Anyhow, my good friend was in the Toluca jail and the government officials said he would stay there for twenty Aprils. This is a long time for only making idols and such for the gringo *turistas*, no?

When I visited with him in the jail, he told me an interesting story. He says that west of Chilpancingo there are two peaks of the Sierra Madre del Sur that are pretty well aligned, north and south. I know these peaks and have often prospected on their slopes. To the north is a large, grassy plain with only a few trees. On this plain there are some mounds, like drumlins or small round hills. My friend, with his fondness for idols and other genuine artifacts and gold, had gone to these small hills with two Indians and some mules to carry their camp gear and any artifacts they might find, as a poor *gambusino* that some people call El Lobo had told him that there

---

[7] El Lobo is putting on an act here, probably as he would do if questioned by authorities concerning his own dealings.

were some old tombs and pyramids far to the west of this vast plain, in the range by the sea. They found these tombs and, having loaded the mules with fine jade idols, were returning over the route by which they had come. They were walking along, leading their mules in the warm Mexican sun and feeling very good about the profitable conclusion of their idol stealing, when they noticed a depression on the side of one of the mounds they were passing. It appeared to be a cave-in caused by the heavy rainy season just past. It turned out to be a hole that went into the mound. They stopped and got their shovels from the mules. Clearing away the soft dirt and grass, they found steps going down into the little hill. After much digging and shifting of boulders, they came to a stone slab, about four feet high and so heavy they couldn't move it. Finally they were able to break it and pry it away and shine their flashlight into the hole, revealing a room beyond. They continued the work of removing the large rock door and at last were able to enter the room, which was about ten feet square and lined with squared stones, fitted together so well that the joints were barely visible.

In this room were many idols, both large and small. Some were of gold, others of clay, and a few of jade. There also were many pots and jars of all sizes, some sealed, others open, containing artifacts, ore, food, and grain. Some had turquoise, some had cinnabar (used for red paint), others had gold, arrow and axe heads, obsidian drills, and other artifacts. One of the gold idols was too big and heavy for the three of them to take from the room. They chopped it up with their machetes and, after unloading the jade idols taken in their previous haul, filled their alforjas with it, the rest of the gold idols, and as much of the loose gold as they could carry. Then they refilled the entrance and smoothed the dirt so that grass might grow and conceal it until they could return for more of the treasure.

My friend told me that beyond the room where they had found the gold idols, through another stone slab door that they had been able to move slightly, were more rooms. With his light he could see that these rooms contained more big idols and pots, and also some figures as tall as a man, perhaps mummies. There probably are more gold idols in this other room, and surely many of stone, clay, and perhaps jade. There also are the jade idols he left in the first room so he could take the gold ones. This man is no liar, for I have known him long and we have been on such trips together. When he says they are there, *they are there*!

They started for Balsas with their heavy loads of gold idols, to go from there to Mexico on the railroad that runs as far as Balsas and stops after it crosses the high iron bridge over the Balsas River.

As they neared the town they heard much shooting, so they buried the gold and went on toward the railroad with their packs empty. When they got to the railroad, they waited until a train came by, and my friend jumped on as it moved slowly up the hill. He left the mules and camp outfit for the two Indians to take care of until he could return with a few trusted friends to recover the gold.

The firing was just some people who did not like the governor of Guerrero, shooting at some others who did. These little wars are not always dangerous to people who are not interested in the local politics, but the participants are not good people to meet when you have much gold and no friends with you, such as our friend Manuel, with his two big pistols that he uses so effectively, and his fine bunch of cattle thieves.

At last my friend was able to return with some trusted associates, but when he got back to Balsas he could find neither his two Indians nor his mules and gear. No one knew what had become of them, and he didn't dare ask too many questions because of the gold. After several days of searching, he went to the place where he had buried the gold idols but found only a hole in the ground. He returned to Mexico, sadder and wiser. His venture had not been totally unprofitable, for he had kept one of the finest gold idols when he had buried the rest. Later the two Indians were found, shot in the back. My friend also learned that they had been seen with a Spaniard, and that he, too, had disappeared.

This gringo friend of mine, who is accused of terrible things such as stealing national treasures that the government didn't even know existed, still has the one small gold idol he took when he buried the others. The *policía* did not find this one, as he had it and some other prized artifacts well hidden. It weighs about two kilos, and the gold is about eight hundred fine. I know that this is all the truth, for I have known this gringo a long time, and I can go to the mounds whenever we wish, for I have seen them many times.

They put this man in jail and charged him with stealing over a million dollars worth of idols in the last ten years. They also accused him of killing the two Indians, as well as stealing millions of dollars worth of idols that he had already shipped out of the country, but all they thought they actually could prove was about a million dollars' worth of the stuff that they confiscated from his *bodega*.

The Spaniard, if there was a Spaniard, will never come back. He probably didn't find out where the gold idols had been found. The Indians probably took him to the cache on the promise of a few pesos and all the mescal they could drink, and got themselves shot for their trouble. My good friend may have shot them himself. *¿Quién sabe?* I know what some of the generals I have known would have done for a lot less than two mule loads of gold. He might have figured there was no more need of them and, alive, they had to be fed. It also was time to pay them, and there was no more digging to be done. Besides these two knew too much. But what really happened is anybody's guess.

All this is true. It is not a wild tale of some witch doctor or other Indian, trying to promote a job to guide someone to look for treasure. My friend told me all this because he will never dare go back again. If he gets out of jail, he will try to go to England and will not return to Mother Mexico soon. If he cannot get out of the country, he will be so closely watched that it would be impossible for him to do anything but attend strictly to his legitimate business. He wished me to know all of this because I have many times given him information that led him to profitable finds. He also told me just how to find the opening to the stone room, where he left all of the jade idols. When the time is right, I shall go to this place, I think.

PART THREE

Gold and Revolution

The years that El Lobo prospected and mined gold in the Sonora Desert of northwestern Mexico, I am sure, were the happiest he had ever known, and he lived them to the full. He loved his Yaquis, and especially his Yaqui wife, Puñalita, but still one place and one woman could never hold him permanently. He was born to wander—to see the other side of the mountain, and to follow the call of the gold that lay in the hills mas allá, *farther on. He had a great zest for life and never seemed to spend a lot of time looking back; yet I often felt that he regretted, far more than he admitted, having thrown away what he loved most for the adventure to be found in revolution and intrigue.*

Between his adventures—of flying planes to revolutionaries, or prospecting elsewhere in Mexico and other parts of Latin America—he occasionally returned to Sonora and the Yaquis. One such homecoming, which lasted a year, was prompted by his need for a place to rest and recover from illness and injuries suffered in a plane crash, others, perhaps, by a need for a place to hide.

His companion on many of these adventures was a woman. The relationship that existed between them, whether or not it was exactly as he described it, was, by almost any standard, unique. They were alike in many ways. His characterization of her—wild and unpredictable—could be applied to himself as well. One of their adventures involved flying aircraft to General Saturnino Cedillo—already introduced. Another, at a later time, concerned flying and prospecting in Honduras. But the story is his, and he should tell it.

13

Rebecca

I HAD MANY FINE ADVENTURES with a beautiful Jewish girl —I'll just call her Rebecca—who was the daughter of a family friend. She was always like my sister; I would not care to hurt her. But if she should ever see any of the stories you might write, she will be mad enough to cut my throat. What a temper that gal had!

She was worth about thirty million dollars. Her father and my father and uncle had been close friends and business associates. Before she was born, my father had helped her father, starting him on the way to his millions. She was wild, unpredictable, and didn't know the meaning of fear. Her family could do nothing with her. She had a burning desire to learn to fly, and her father knew that it would be only a

matter of days until she killed herself in a rented plane; so
he turned her over to me to teach her what little I knew about
flying. He knew I would at least do my best to keep her from
getting herself killed and thought she might tame down a
little in Mexico with my wife and me.[1] The old millionaire
did me great honor with his confidence, but taking care of his
headstrong daughter was no easy job.

When she first started to fly, shortly after World War I, I
was ferrying aircraft for a small, badly managed aircraft
sales company that bought and sold all kinds of flying junk,
and believe me, the U.S.A. was full of junk aircraft in those
days. Many ships were no good, even when they were new.
Some had spin troubles or structural defects that you found
out about at ten thousand feet over rough mountains in turbulent air. Some of these early planes were really wonderful
ships, but others were pure dynamite. The company I was
flying for bought ships of any kind, fixed them up with paint
and dope, and sold them to customers in Mexico, Central
America, South America, China, or wherever they could find
a buyer. There were many wartime military ships in use, and
also many war-surplus engines that were used in civilian ships
built after the war. These were mostly new engines, but still
wartime engines. The best were not too good, but we used to
improve on them in many ways: by raising the compression,
installing better and more piston rings, improving oil control,
and using better spark plugs and German Bosch and the new
Scintilla Swiss magnetos, which were hotter. The Liberty
twelve-cylinder V-type, water-cooled engine, Curtiss, Hispano
Suiza V-eight, and a Navy engine with dual ignition all were
used on "new production" aircraft, as the postwar ships were
called. The Hispano Suiza engines were particularly liked by

[1] The reference here is not to El Lobo's Yaqui wife. He had three
wives first and last, including an American woman who lived in West
Texas, and a Mexican woman of Mexico City, who bore him a son.

the Mexican and other Spanish American generals. They liked them in Wacos and other ships. The Hisso-Waco was most popular in Mexico. We called it the Mexican Pursuit. This engine had powered the French Spad during the war, and many were used in American airplanes after the war.

When I was flying for this company, I handled all types of ships, as I delivered them everywhere and flew trade-ins back to our shops. I also brought to the company's airport planes purchased for rebuilding or overhaul, for resale. I had more nerve than brains in those days. I wanted to build up hours in all types of aircraft. I received no regular pay, just expenses. I got lots of flying time, besides seeing much of both North and South America.

My father and my uncle long before had given me up as worthless. They had wanted me to go to college, then take care of their mines and railroad properties, and settle down as a man of means should and stay away from airplanes. I did like railroading, especially running and repairing locomotives, but I was too hard-headed to listen to them.

I ran into some strange deals and strange people on this crazy job, and it was while I was in this work that Rebecca flew with me for the first time. Having bought a new airplane and received her ten-hour private license, she wanted to learn all she could about flying. I had a reputation, even then, as an adventurer and pilot. People thought I was a wild, reckless, and wonderful pilot. None of this was true, for I was only a fair pilot and not at all wild and reckless, but very careful.[2]

I was a hell of a coward, very much afraid of falling and of

[2] Only in a sense was he a careful pilot. He meticulously checked out his plane before take-off, and he was fully aware of the dangers of flying. He knew how to handle a plane and knew just what each ship he flew was capable of doing—and often pushed it near the limit. And frequently he flew with enough liquor in him to cause him to be reckless.

fire, but to Rebecca I was a brave pilot and a big hero. She asked me if she could not pay me to let her take a few trips with me. Besides wanting to learn to fly many types of ships, she wanted to learn more about Mexico and other Latin American countries. She said she was now over eighteen and was her own boss and had her own bank account. She wanted to know how much I would charge her per trip.

Not above taking advantage of her innocence in business dealings, I struck a bargain whereby she would pay all expenses when we were flying—hers and mine—and buy me all the rum I could drink besides, however much it might take to stop the damned engines from running in my head. She was to do all the copilot's chores—inspecting the ship, wiping the controls and windshield, and checking fuel, lubrication, and water—and do most of the flying after take-off.

My boss almost had apoplexy when he found out who she was, then saw her calling me captain, taking my orders, and working on the oily engines in a tailored suit that must have cost two hundred dollars, while I sat in the plane reading *Esquire*. He tried to get me to marry her for her money, or at least persuade her to back his business.

On our first trip together, we took a Ford Trimotor to Mexico City, and I put her through the paces of flying the big ship. My copilot then wanted to see more of Mexico, and both of us were tired of flying, so we took the train to Guadalajara. After visiting this beautiful and historic city, we bought tickets on El Rápido of the Sud Pacífico de México for Nogales.

The train had an observation car with a shiny brass rail around the rear platform, and we sat back there and drank Carta Blanca and listened to the rails and watched the scenery go by. The old car swayed and groaned and the desert brush swept its sides. Now and then the long, clear whistle of the engine, far ahead, came back to us as we ate and drank. A Mexican Army captain and a couple of gringo school teachers came back to the observation platform, so I went forward to the third class cars and rounded up four mariachis to play and sing for us. We had a fine party. I paid off the entertainers before we all went in to the diner.

The Mexican captain said he would give us a party that evening, and sent a brakeman forward to tell the mariachi to come back to the end car again. We spent a very enjoyable evening, drinking and listening to the old songs of Mexico and Spain. The mariachi also had a very good time and after every 2 or 3 songs they would drink a bottle of our beer, seasoned with a big shot of mescal. I noticed that the one who appeared to be the leader marked each song on his cuff. At about 2 o'clock, we decided to go to bed and the American girls left to go to their car. I thanked the captain for the fine evening's entertainment and started to leave. He turned to the musicians and asked how much he owed them. They figured up the bill at 175 pesos.

"What! A hundred and seventy five pesos after eating our food and drinking our beer and liquor all night! *Bandidos*! I won't pay you anything for trying to cheat me!" The Indians pulled their knives and started to circle the captain. He drew his Colt forty-five and it looked as though we would have some more good Mexican entertainment to finish up the evening.

The conductor ran off, and Rebecca cried, "Stop them! Stop them! I'll pay them. Don't fight over a little money! Someone will get hurt!" She was too late, however, for the captain shot one of them through the shoulder and the others jumped off the train. It was only going about twenty-five miles an hour, so maybe they didn't get killed; it's pretty hard to kill a drunken Indian. After the shooting, the captain opened another bottle of beer and drank it, then went to sleep on the floor with the man he had just shot. ¡*Viva México*!

I told my copilot to think nothing of it. Just a little Mexican fun. Things like that happened all the time. We went forward to our berths and turned in for what was left of the night. I think maybe Rebecca was learning more about Mexico than she had bargained for. Next morning the captain joined us for breakfast, joking and smiling, and nothing was said about the shooting.

We were on the train three days before arriving at the border. After clearing customs we took a bus to Tucson, then again boarded a train to the home field. Rebecca said that she had learned more on that one flight than in all the time she had spent in flying school. She made many trips with me after that. She was a very nice and proper girl with all kinds of guts. But she could be mean as hell, and dangerous.

For a long time after I had married Puñalita, she didn't know quite how to take Rebecca. But she finally came to accept her, and we had some good times together. It was always tit-for-tat with Rebecca and me, and that's what Puñalita didn't understand. Rebecca had a habit of going off half cocked and, when she did, I handed her back as much hell as she gave.

Rebecca was always fascinated by mines—or anything else that offered the prospect of money. Once she went with us to La Mina Gran Provendera del Cobre, which I then owned. It was about seventeen miles south of Caborca. There are several old mines in the group, located in the northern part of the range on a pretty big mountain. There is a steep inclined shaft, about 550 feet deep, and many underground workings.

This property has both copper and gold. Southeast of the shaft about three miles are the ruins of two smelters. One is

Spanish and very old, but the other probably is French, German, or English—maybe American. All this had been abandoned during the great revolution, and the owners had never returned. There were several water-jacket Marcy furnaces there when I found the place. A short distance from the inclined shaft is another deep shaft, which I never did attempt to get down into. I found much rich silver ore on the surface around this old shaft.

Farther south there is another group of old workings. I owned all of these properties in those days but let them go for taxes. I never did get any of them completely explored, but when I was working in the mine with the deep inclined shaft, we found a drift that had been walled up, and I reopened it. We found a large quantity of turquoise, already mined and graded, hidden in the walled-up tunnel. I don't know whether it had come out of La Mina Gran Provendera or just been taken there for hiding. I did not find any turquoise during my exploration. I wasn't interested in turquoise, so I gave it all to my Indians. They value it highly.

There is a good gold property about four or five miles south of Noria. It was burned out during Villa's time and has not been worked since. I have found good ore in part of the workings, but I believe a new shaft would have to be sunk to enter the main workings safely and to strike the best ore. The Indians all call this mine Las Ánimas, which means ghosts and spirits, because the *gambusinos* all believe this mine to be haunted. I don't know what it was called before the revolution, when it was still being worked and before it was wrecked and burned and all the people killed. Las Ánimas is a good name for it now. Strange things happen when you go underground into the old workings, and many strange sounds are often heard. I have heard some of these ghostly sounds myself. Away down there in the lonely dark drifts you seem to hear men talking in Spanish, and sometimes even in English. In another place you plainly hear a man groaning and begging for water in Spanish.

One time we were in this old mine trying to figure out how to hoist from one of the drifts where I had opened up some high-grade ore so that we could get the ore to the surface and take it to my mill at La Ciénaga. We were eating our lunch, Puñalita sitting on one side of me, Rebecca on the other.

There we sat, deep underground in a dangerous, burned out old gold mine—a gringo prospector between a wild Yaqui wife and a millionaire's wild daughter, and a lot of my wife's half-tamed Yaqui relations squatting on the floor of the drift in front of us—a damn fine wild crew to have around, especially underground. Rebecca was not only headstrong, but wild and mean and given to fits of temper. She carried a gun and would use it. Puñalita, with her long, sharp knife, was pretty much the same. Either one would shoot, stab, and cut when she got mad. It was always best to make yourself scarce when that happened.

I was sitting there mulling over my problems and eating dried venison and frijoles when the carbide lamp went out. We had brought only one that would work, so while one of my *gambusinos* tried to fix it in the dark, I went through my pockets for matches (the flint lighter had been lost from the lamp long before).

It was pitch dark and very still. Suddenly we heard, far off down the dark and spooky drift, "¡*Agua, agua, por favor, agua!*" The Yaqui *gambusinos* froze, and all work on the lamp stopped. I could hear their heavy breathing. The eerie cry was repeated, trailing off into a long, drawn-out moan. It sure didn't sound good, down deep in the old mine without lights. Then I struck a match to the carbide lamp, and we had light again. Suddenly Rebecca hauled off and hit me on the mouth.

"Keep your dirty paws off my hair, damn you!" she said.

My wife gave me a dirty look for, although she spoke no English, she was just a little jealous of the white girl.

I was puzzled. I told Rebecca, "I never touched you, and if you hit me like that again I'll tie you up and leave you down here, you New York bitch!"

"You pulled my hair and ran your hands through it!"

"No, I didn't touch you. I was too busy trying to get the lamp going again."

We let it go at that and, after we had finished eating, went on down the drift. We came to a deep winze that seemed to go right down to hell—or even deeper. It was on an incline and not too steep, so we worked our way slowly and carefully down it. As we went deeper, we found that stone steps had been cut along the foot wall, and there were old "chicken ladders," or notched logs that the Indians use for ladders. These logs were so old they crumbled in our hands, but I had plenty of rope, so we made an end fast and slid down it.

Pretty soon Rebecca started complaining again that someone was pulling her hair. I told her to shut up, no one was touching her. Suddenly she let out a howl and wrapped her arms around me, knocking the lamp from my hand, and it went out again. Again we were in the deep dead darkness of the old mine, in much worse shape than the first time. The lamp had rolled and the Yaquis crawled around on the floor, trying to find it.

Rebecca was hysterical. "Save me! Save me!" she cried.

"Well," I said, "you seem to be all here, just what do you want me to do?"

Then she screamed again. "It's got me! It's *got* me!"

"What's got you?"

"The ghost! The ghost! It's got me! Oh, won't someone save me?"

Now I am a very big coward myself, and I did not like this dangerous old mine because I knew that, in its condition, it could cave and crush us most any time, but I was drawn to it because I knew it still had lots of high-grade ore. I like to explore old mines, but I knew the danger. This fear had worked on me until I was a bit jumpy, especially after everything that had happened. I yelled at Rebecca, "For God's sake, woman, let go of me! The thing probably doesn't want me, give me a chance to run!" She was squeezing the breath right out of me.

"Oooh," she screamed again, "don't leave me! Save me from this thing!" I believe that I would have left, light or no light, if I could have got loose from her.

My poor Indians at last found the lamp and began working on it, trying to get it started again. It was lucky they didn't know English, for if they had understood what we said they would have spooked for sure. Then we really would have been in trouble. At last the lamp popped and flared.

In Rebecca's hair was one of the biggest bats I had ever seen. He was just sitting there, with that tired look that all mine bats seem to have. I carefully lifted him off her head and placed him on a high rock. That was one of the ghosts of Las Ánimas, but I still don't know what makes the strange sounds and voices down there deep in the old underground workings.

¿Quién sabe, amigo, quién sabe?

Once while I had my mill at La Ciénaga, I took Puñalita, Rebecca, and a young fellow who worked for me as bartender in my little cantina on a fishing trip to Tiburón Island. I hired a fishing boat to take us to Tiburón, a dry desert island in the Mar de Cortés (Gulf of California) about half a mile off the Sonora coast. It has many caves and some old mine workings.

We drove over to a fishing village on the coast in one of my dump trucks. It was about fifty miles over very bad roads. I had a good double-barreled shotgun and a couple of boxes of shells, with a few more in my pocket. Planning to stay on the island at least five days and do some exploring and hunting, we had bedrolls, water, grub, and prospecting gear. The fishing boat captain unloaded our gear, and I made arrangements for him to come back for us in five days.

There were lots of ducks on the island, so I shot several, cleaned them, and laid them near our bedrolls. We planned to do some prospecting next day. Before I turned in, I discovered that the only shells I had were the few in my pocket; the two full boxes had been left in the truck on the mainland.

We each had bedrolls and Puñalita slept on one side of me, Rebecca on the other. My bartender slept off to himself. The moon was very large and beautiful over the wild Sonora desert, and the rough mountain ranges stood out plainly in the bright moonlight. Tiburón Island is a weird, wild place in the daytime and, at night in the moonlight, it is still more lonely and wild looking. The smooth tropic sea was peaceful; the small waves made little sound on the flat, sandy beach. The steep, sharp mountain peaks on the island looked like mountains on the moon. It is a beautiful, quiet land.

We were all tired and went to sleep at once. About midnight some sound startled me awake. I sat up in my blankets and looked around. The big moon had set and it was now very dark. Then I heard a noise not far away and turned my flashlight in its direction. Just a short distance away was a circle of eyes. Everywhere I turned the light, the eyes glowed. Then I heard snarling and gnashing of teeth, then some crunching of bones. Whatever was out there was eating something. I kicked Puñalita awake and showed her the glowing eyes, but she just covered up her head. Then I kicked Rebecca; she took a long look, then dove under the covers. Then I got up and kicked my bartender; he groaned and at last got up, but when he saw what was out there, he also hid under his blankets. I picked up the shotgun and fired at some of the eyes and the animals all ran off. When I went to see about our ducks, they were gone. I had only four more shells, so I too went back to sleep. What else could I do? These animals must have been big wolves, or wild dogs, judging by the tracks we found next morning. Each night we were there they came and sat around us, but they did not come as near as they had that first night.

Tiburón Island is an interesting place to explore. It has a good runway, about a mile long. Many smugglers land there to pick up gold, and fishing boats come to the island to land contraband. There are giant manta rays around the island, some more than twenty-five feet across from tip to tip of their outside wings. The gulf has many whales, both blues and big blacks. We saw many giant sea turtles and large sharks, some as long as thirty-five feet, and many big octopuses. The small octopus is good eating, and so is the young shark.

Sometime after this fishing trip, I bought a twenty-six-foot sloop-rigged whaleboat powered by a one-cylinder gasoline engine. I sailed her all over the Mar de Cortés. There are some sunken ships along the Sonora coast, and all kinds of stories center around them. On the southern end of Tiburón there are lots of copper showings and some of gold. A small mountain range lies inland. If you are ever there and need water, there is a good beach of white sand and, back about two hundred yards from the beach, is a large sand flat. You can dig about two feet down in this sand and find fair water. There are lots of animal diggings there, with bones and shells lying around them. Many shipwrecked people have died on Tiburón Island because they didn't know about this water. The Sonora shore is dry and desolate for many miles inland at this point. The caves on Tiburón have been lived in for thousands of years, and there are many artifacts to be found by digging in the floors of these old caves.

A lot of ships went into the Mar de Cortés in the old days by mistake and got into all kinds of trouble. There is a story of a big treasure from a shipwreck buried on the island. This vessel was a wooden side-wheeler rigged as a four-masted bark that had come from South America carrying gringo and Canadian passengers going home from a South American mining boom. She was far off course, the navigators probably thinking they were in the open sea, when she caught fire near Tiburón. The ship ran aground on the south end of the island, and there she burned in shallow water. Some say the crew got the gold out and buried it on the island, others that the gold is still in the hulk. Most of the people aboard died because they tried to find a town by walking inland. There is nothing inland for many miles, and at this time the Seri Indians were even more dangerous than they are now—and they are plenty bad today. The Indans killed a lot of the survivors, too. The Mexican government has killed off a lot of the Seri and sickness has diminished their numbers further, so that now there are only a few hundred left. They travel and fish in strange-looking boats, canoe-shaped with high bow and stern, and big enough for eight or ten oarsmen.[3]

[3] The Seri probably inhabited the Baja California peninsula before they came to the Sonora coast to settle in the vicinity of Tiburón Island, as they have marked cultural differences from their present neighbors. Although they were brought under mission influence briefly in the eighteenth century, the attempt was unsuccessful. They rose in revolt against the Spaniards in 1748, which was complicated in 1751 by the Pima uprising. Even after the Pima rebellion was suppressed, intermittent hostilities by the Seri continued, and they were still a menace when the Marqués de Rubí arrived in Sonora in 1767. Despite the missionaries' efforts, the Seri returned to their old nomadic life on the coast, leading an independent existence into the middle twentieth century, with only minor alterations in their traditional social and religious life. Their population has declined steadily, however, and their number in the late 1960's was slightly more than three hundred. Since 1930 they have engaged in independent commercial fishing.

Off the south end of the island, in about twenty feet of water, we found the wrecks of two old ships. One was a very old sailing vessel with a high poop deck. She had been quite large, about 175 to 200 feet long. Jammed into a sort of coral or lime formation, she was thickly covered with a gray-white rock-like sediment. From this wreck we took three cannon, one of brass and two of iron. We also got some large pulley blocks, made of a heavy black wood and thickly crusted with lime. She may have been one of the old Spanish Philippine fleet. The other wreck was a steamer, and we found four of her boilers; it may have been the old side-wheeler. She was far gone in rot and badly broken up.

Exploring old shipwrecks is even more dangerous than entering old mines. Sharks were bad around these wrecks.

All this happened a long time ago, before World War II, when life in Mexico was easy and good. There probably will never be such a good life again.

Indirectly, the good times we had vacationing and exploring around Tiburón Island caused an incident that very nearly cost Rebecca and me our lives. We were flying a nearly new Taylorcraft south along the west coast of Mexico, delivering it to a Mexican buyer. On our route, the sand hills along the Sonora coast came right up to the beach. We were flying just above the water along this wild and desolate coast, with nothing in sight but the beach and only sand and desert for many miles inland. This is the range of the wild and dangerous Seri Indians, who often kill prospectors and fishermen and eat them. They are real cannibals.[4] The Mexican government has tried to exterminate them, but Tiburón Island and the beach both north and south of Tiburón are wild. In addition to the

[4] References to such cannibalism at this time are lacking in the scant literature dealing with the Seri, although ceremonial cannibalism was practiced among the Uto-Aztecans and Cahitans in earlier times.

cannibal Seris, there are the large wolves that often kill men. This is a wild, lonely, dangerous place to find yourself without supplies or weapons.

Flying very low along the beach, we could see many beautifully colored shells cast up by the tide. The beach was wide and extended for miles and miles and, like the damned fool that I usually am, I was seized by a sudden impulse to land. The ship rolled along on the wet sand until she slowed down, and then she started to sink in. We came very close to nosing over. Almost afraid to learn how bad the situation was, we climbed out and looked about us. It was lonely and desolate. With the tide at flood, we stood there as the sea came to the ship and the wheels settled even more.

"Quick!" I snapped, "help me move her!" Rebecca lifted and pushed on one side, I on the other. Together we were just able to move the ship up on the beach enough to get her out of the sea wash. Climbing one of the big sand dunes, we could see nothing inland but sand. Nothing grew; there was no water. We were the only living things in sight, but in the sand at our feet were the huge tracks, about $4\frac{1}{2}$ inches across, of one of the big wolves, and they looked fresh.

I looked at Rebecca, and she looked at me and said, "You damn fool! You have done it now! We will die here. The ship can't fly out of this sand."

"Guess you are right, copilot," I said. Let's go and pick up some pretty shells anyway. Then we can try to find a hard place on the beach where we might be able to take off."

Walking along the beach, we found a much harder surface about a quarter of a mile away. I tied the stick back so the tail of the plane wouldn't rise up and throw her on her back, and both of us pushed. An airplane is hard to handle this way. Now and then, as we moved along slowly, a gust of wind would catch under a wing or under her tail and she would nearly get away from us. The hot Sonora sun beat down on

us. We had only a small bottle of water, which we didn't dare
drink because we didn't know whether we were going to be
able to fly or not. But finally, with both of us lifting and pushing for all we were worth and, with the help of the little
sixty-five-horsepower Continental engine, we managed to get
the plane to the harder beach.

Rebecca's being a millionaire, it made me laugh to see her
all sweaty and lifting and pushing the plane. I helped her out
by telling her stories of how the Seri Indians ate fishermen
and that they had a special fondness for Jews. I told her I
knew the old Seri chief, and he had told me that Jews tasted
just like pork. This made her mad as hell, and she threatened
to shoot me on the spot and came damn near doing it, too.
This I thought very funny, because it looked like we were
going to die anyway, out there without water and with the
big wolves close at hand. I thought the ship probably would
nose over on take-off and break the little wooden prop, and
that would be it. Then the big wolves or wild dogs, or whatever they are, would eat us sure—if the damn Seris didn't get
to us first.

We would carry the airplane a little way in the 125 to
130-degree heat and then lie in the shade of the wing to rest.
While we were resting I would tell her anything I could think
of to make her mad. When her feet started to bleed from all
the hard work in the sand, lifting and pushing the ship, I
told her that now the big wolves would smell blood and be
down on us for sure. She more than half believed me and was
getting scared. Then I told her that if the Seris came, I could
fix things so that they wouldn't kill us and put us in the pot.
She wanted to know how.

"Well," I said, "I know the old chief, so I will tell him that
I came here to sell him a woman. This way I can save myself
and you will become one of the chief's wives. This is much
better than getting eaten up." This really made her mad.

At last we got to the harder part of the beach, away from the quicksand. We climbed in and opened the throttle. The engine roared, but the ship wouldn't move. I told Rebecca to push and I would try to get her rolling. She pushed and I did my best to get her under way, and we began to move. Faster and faster we taxied along the beach. With Rebecca running as fast as she could, I yelled at her to get in. She made a wild grab at the steel tube back of the windshield and caught it with one hand. Then she started to slip off and I reached over and got hold of her long hair, handling the ship with one hand, trying to pull her in with the other. We were airborne by then, and she would have been a goner if she had fallen. The wind was trying to drag her out, but at last she made it into the plane, exhausted and with bleeding feet. She was a good girl—lots of guts. When she got her breath, she really gave me hell.

I am very proud of Rebecca. She is my most famous student, and I have taught quite a few people to fly. She became about the best of all of them. Some of my old students are now colonels in the Mexican, U.S., and Canadian air forces. A few are U.S. Navy pilots, and some fly for the best airlines. Most of my old students are still alive. In fact, none of them that took much flying with me is dead. I put the fear of airplanes into them and made them careful.

14

Planes for Revolution

I WAS FLYING for General Saturnino Cedillo when he had his revolution and also before. I drilled water wells on his ranch and prospected for mercury for him for a long time, and we were good friends for many years.

General Cedillo was governor of the state of San Luis Potosí. When he started his small revolution he needed aircraft, so I helped him get some.[5] One was a Speedwing Travelair, another a Taperwing Waco with a 180-horsepower Hisso engine. Then there was another big Travelair with a 3-6-9 Wright engine, and some others. The general also had some Spartan low-wing, all-metal cabin monoplanes. He had a good gringo chief pilot and a good Mexican chief mechanic. I did not fly

[5] See note 5, part II.

combat much. The general used me mostly for his contact man to get aircraft. He couldn't get clearance because the *federales* knew what he was up to and watched him closely. I had to find pilots who would climb in and fly south with a ship and deliver it to him at his capital-city stronghold of San Luis Potosí without worrying about clearance, or else I had to fly them to him myself. After they delivered the ships to him, these pilots could either join up with his air force at good pay or return to the States.

Rebecca, by now, was in the aircraft business herself. She had rented a big hangar on a nice airfield in the Midwest and was buying and selling aircraft of all kinds. Although she was rich, she still liked to turn an easy dollar when she could. By this time she could fly better than I, and she no longer saw fit to pay my expenses and buy my rum. She now found it better just to keep me on a salary and pay me a commission on any ships I sold. She had got what she wanted—lots of experience flying and navigating and a knowledge of how to get along in Latin America.

One bright and balmy spring morning, when I asked her if she wanted to make some fast dollars, she looked long and hard at me, her mouth drawn tight, and said, "Well?"

"Now look, Rebecca," I said, "I have some valuable information. In fact, this information and my connection are priceless. It has cost me a lot of time and money to get this information and I am going to use it. Do you want to help me?"

She just looked at me for about a minute, then said, "How much will all this cost me?"

"Cost you? Cost you?" I yelled. "The information is not for sale at any price. But you may cash in on it and not even know about it."

"We were in her hangar and she was dressed in flying clothes, ready to take a student up for a flying lesson. She was surrounded by her pilots and mechanics and hangers-on—all

of them trying to sell her something or marry her, and resent-
ting me, for none of them could get anywhere with her. But
she and I would just climb into a ship and she would tell her
chief pilot, "Take care of things, I will be gone for a while."
And sometimes it was *quite* a while. They all thought it was
love, but it was only money and experience that she was after.

This nice bright day, her people were all ears and crowded
around close to hear what was said. I looked around, laughed,
and said, "Rebecca, send some of your pilots up with the
students. I cannot talk here. With a Cuba Libre in my hand
I can do this deal full justice."

Her eyes flashed fire and she said, "My student is on land-
ings, and is about to go solo. I can't leave now, but when I get
back I will talk with you."

"No!" I said. "Send a pilot with your student. I am ready
to speak with you now, not tomorrow. Do you want to make
some big money quick or don't you?"

That did it. She sent a pilot up with the student and gave
orders to her pilots and mechanics. None of them was pleased,
but they took the orders. She asked me if she should change
her clothes.

"No, copilot," I laughed. With a dirty look, she followed
me to her new Duesenberg Speedster, a model called the
Twenty Grand. It was a big straight eight with double over-
head camshafts, dual ignition, and supercharger, with 330
horsepower—same as a 3-6-9 Wright engine. I climbed in like
I owned it and fired her up. This was something only I could
do. After all, wasn't I her first chief pilot? She would never
let her other pilots or anyone else drive her Duesie, but she
always told me to drive.

She got in and said, "Shall I call you captain or mister?
You said that I had to do as you say and just as you say, so!"

"It will be captain again, Rebecca."

We stopped at a bar and went in where there was soft

music and little light. She ordered the drinks and said, "Well?"

I looked to make sure that no one could hear us and said, "It is like this, Rebecca, you must trust me quite a bit now, but it will be worth it. You need to know no more than I say here. In fact, it is better that you know nothing. Do you know the Speedwing Travelair called the *Golden Flash*?"

"Yes, what about it?"

I told her that this airplane could be bought for $10,000 cash. "I want to buy it and fly it to Mexico and sell it. For this job you will get $5,000, but you must buy the ship today and put her papers in the mail for Washington as it should be done—then she will vanish." This ship was well worth $15,000, but to General Cedillo she was priceless. She was very fast and maneuverable for her day, a real stunt ship. She was powered by a 3-6-9 Wright that had had more than $20,000 spent on it—special steel in the rods and crankshaft, special alloy in her bearings, special alloy pistons. She had a high gear ratio in her supercharger and, with all this and her special valves and high-dome pistons, she developed much more than her rated horsepower of 330 and could stand much higher RPM than any other 3-6-9. She also had gun synchronizers as standard factory equipment, as often these engines were bought for military use. The ship had won many cross-country races and had been completely rebuilt.

"How do you know that you can sell this Travelair?" Rebecca asked. "I don't want that white elephant and I need the ten thousand just now."

"I know because I know," I said, "and I could sell many more of the same kind of ship if we could get them."

Rebecca looked at me sideways and asked, "How many more?"

"Just as many more as you or I can find, but they must be perfect, like this plane is, or I don't want them. I am buying airplanes, not junk, and I can get top price for anything that I buy. Hey, bartender, another Cuba Libre!"

"All right," she said. "What shall I make the check out for?"

"Just make it out for the ten thousand in full for one Travelair Speedwing. Here is her number. We are buying as is and where is FAF [fly-away field]. Then there will be my expenses or, shall we say, the captain's fund? That will be another five hundred in advance. You will receive an order on the Chase National Bank in New York City for fifteen thousand when I say the word. And we can sell some more ships if we work fast."

She was writing checks now and was all business. I ordered another drink and pocketed my check. I was making things as cheap as I could for General Cedillo. The ship would have cost him twice as much any other way. Down there in San Luis, with the *federales* watching all the time for ships being smuggled in, she was priceless.

When she had finished the check writing and I had finished my drink, I said, "Well, let's go and take delivery now." We drove to an airport on the other side of town, after phoning the wealthy oil man who owned the *Golden Flash* and telling him to meet us at the hangar.

He was there, and we finished transferring the papers at once. He knew both of us, and was curious. "Now what? Going out for a cross-country record in my ship? You had better watch your step, girl. You will bust your butt in this plane. She is nothing to fool with."

"No," said Rebecca, "I am not going out for any records, I am not even going to fly the ship. My pilot here is going to fly her."

"Do you think he can handle her?" the oil man asked. "It takes an aviator to fly this ship and stay alive."

"Well, he is going to try," she told him. "Fill her up with gas and oil; we should get something for our cash deal."

I told her that I would need helmet and goggles, and asked if I might have hers.

"No," she said, "I'm going with you. Do you think I want to miss the fun?" The oil man gave me his helmet and goggles, then plied us with more questions. "Where are you two going? Is this a honeymoon or elopement? What goes on, anyway?"

Rebecca replied coolly, "This is business, mister, and we are going quite a long way if this old wreck of yours will fly."

The mechanics now were cleaning off the windshields on the two open cockpits and wiping the wings and fuselage. I had inspected the ship carefully and drained her sediment bulbs early that morning, and I was in a hurry. Matters were going too smoothly, and I wanted to be gone before it changed. The front cockpit had a seat for two people, and complete instrument panel and controls. The rear cockpit was intended for the pilot, but she could be flown from either. There was an electric telephone between the two cockpits for communication between pilot and navigator on cross-country flights. She was loaded with expensive instruments and all the navigation instruments of her day—drift indicator, artificial horizon, and two compasses. She was a pilot's dream.

The Wright engine now was running, as a mechanic was warming her up. Rebecca asked if she could park her car in the hangar until we got back.

"You sure can, Rebecca, but where in hell are you going?" he asked.

"Just for a little ride, mister, that's all," she told him. She took her heavy flying coat out of her car and put it on over her flying suit. Rebecca settled into the front seat, and I got into the rear cockpit. The hushed murmur of the idling

Wright engine and the clatter of her noisy valves came back to me in the comfortable, deep seat.

The mechanic leaned close to my head as I adjusted my goggles and said, "She is full of gas and she is really heavy. She has extra large gas tanks and also her center section is full of gas. You have over a thousand miles in those tanks. Watch the red marks on the instruments. You can't hurt that engine if you keep her inside the red lines. Cruising at 2100 RPM won't hurt her."

I appreciated the information from a man who knew the ship well, and said, "Thanks a lot, sir, I'll keep her inside the red lines and do the best I can with her." As he jerked the chocks free, I eased the throttle open and she leaped eagerly ahead. I looked to see if the gas valves were on and, as I taxied, checked the wing tanks and center-section gas gauges.

By the time we reached the end of the long main runway, the engine was warm. I checked the two magnetos and swung her slowly around to look for traffic. As I came into line with the runway, I released her brakes and slowly opened the throttle. The prop was in low pitch, the mixture rich, the spark advanced. She didn't hesitate like some ships do. She became a wild bitch right now. At first she wouldn't answer her rudder—one of her little ways—then she did and was far too fast on it. I had to hold her with the brakes until she was moving fast and also use some stick on her ailerons to keep her on the runway. With all that gas in the upper wings she had a high center of gravity, and she wanted to ground-loop on take-off. All this passed in a flash and she was nice to handle as soon as her tail was up. She tore off down the runway at ninety-five miles per hour, but her wings didn't want to lift her yet. The throttle was jammed against the red throttle stop and all hell seemed to break loose up in front in that nine-cylinder engine. We had used more than half the length of the runway by now. My butt had sprouted teeth and they were chewing at the seat cushion. I didn't know what would happen if I unlatched the throttle stop and shoved it the rest of the way open, but I did know what would happen if I didn't become airborne soon. So I unlatched the throttle stop and jammed her all the way open. She screamed terribly with the prop in low pitch, and her stick became useful—that nice hard feeling that tells you she will answer and fly. I brought the stick back just a little and she was up and gone, faster than I had ever flown.

We gained altitude like a homesick angel in a big, wide turn, and I thumbed her back to the red line and she still seemed to have plenty of climb. I cut her back to 2100 RPM and headed for Mexico, far, far away. The country changed rapidly—much faster than in anything I had ever flown. She cut the air like a sharp machete. I took a deep breath and leaned back. I figured that I might as well enjoy myself now, because I knew I would be very busy when I had to land this wild goose. She didn't have enough gas for a nonstop hop, so we would have to land for gas. I did not dare land near the border, and to land in Mexico before we were in the general's country would be suicidal. At Roswell, New Mexico, we circled high, then let down slowly. I was a little afraid of this field, as it was mostly just open country with piles of old tin cans and other junk on it, but it was big, and that was what I needed. I was very much afraid of what the ship would do when she got her two streamlined wheels down and all the lift was gone from the wings. I knew from the amount of gas we had used so far that there was plenty of range in her tanks to take us from Roswell to San Luis.

At last I got my heart slowed down and my legs quit shaking, so I lined her up with the runway just to see how things looked. We came down low and dragged the field, and it looked a lot better than I had expected. It also looked blurred from our speed. The old fear came back, stronger than before.

I made a big, careful turn, miles in diameter, to get my guts back, and came on in. I knew that she would be blind after her tail was on the ground, so figured I had better get all the lining up done before she dropped her tail. I figured her stick and rudder probably would be dead and I would have to do a lot of braking and rudder fanning.

I put the prop in low pitch, mixture full rich, and shoved my goggles up above my eyes; we came in as the Hamilton Standard prop changed pitch. She snarled like a mad dog, and my heart almost stopped. The desert came up like a brown wall, tearing by beneath us. There were no obstructions at either end of the field, but if she struck rough ground she might cartwheel and burn. I could almost smell the smoke and feel my tender meat burning when I thought of it. I cut the gun and she dropped into a three-point with that good heavy feel that tells you she will stay on the ground and not balloon or bounce. I went after her rudder and brakes like a wild man, as the little sheetiron hangar went by and I started breathing again. I now dared to look around a bit more and we were almost stopped. "Got away with it again!" I thought. I wiped the sweat out of my eyes, turned the ship, and taxied back to the gas pump, feeling very weak and somewhat sick.

It was now late afternoon, so we tied the ship down. It probably was the first time she had ever spent a night out in the open. She was a very special airplane, the pet of a wealthy oil man, and had always been hangared and kept clean. But life was changing for her now. In the luggage compartment I found her tailor-made engine cover and put it on to keep the desert dust and sand out of the nickel-plated engine.

There was an old man in charge of the gas pump, an old Stanavo portable pump on two hard-rubber tires, so Rebecca and I wrestled with heavy drums of gas, and soon had her tanks filled. We then started into town. We had to walk, for there was no transportation. The old man who sold us gas didn't even own a car, and there was no telephone. Walking was nice in the clear desert air of early evening. We had gone only about half a mile when an old rancher in a Model T Ford stopped and gave us a lift into town.

By daylight next morning we were at the field. We were away and gone just as the sun rose. From Roswell to San Luis Potosí is about 850 air miles. With careful handling the Travelair was good for over a thousand miles if we didn't run into headwinds.

There was no stop at the border this time, and we had eighteen thousand feet as we crossed over with a strong tail wind. We had no information about weather, nor did I have charts. At that altitude I was freezing, but I wanted to be high as we crossed into Mexico; and we were high and fast. The sharp cold wind cut through my leather coat like it was paper; my woolen pants were like nothing, and the medium-heavy flying suit I wore didn't turn the cold either. The outside of my helmet was frozen and stiff. As I took a swig from a bottle of Green Dagger rum to ease the chill, the red light on my instrument panel started to flash, indicating my copilot was calling on the cockpit phone.

Rebecca said, "Go down! Go down! I am freezing to death!" We were well into Mexico, over desert-like northern Coahuila, with its scattered rocky ranges of small mountains, dry washes, and big cattle ranches. So I said okay. Soon we were over the timbered range of mountains called Sierra del Venado [Deer Mountains] and a lake showed west of us. I knew we were not far from Torreón. In this part of Mexico we should be safe, for it was controlled by the general, and I began to breathe a lot easier.

Just then I looked up and saw three planes, in formation, off to our right and above us. We had been losing altitude and were now at about nine thousand feet. Were they ships of the general's air force, or were they Mexican Army planes? I took a long hard look. They were coming toward us in an extended dive and were now not more than two miles from us. They were Chance Voughts, and I knew General Cedillo had no Voughts. Then I could see that they were Navy Voughts with Pratt and Whitney Wasp engines. Armed with two thirty-caliber machine guns, they were firing through their props.

I thought the Speedwing should be much faster than the Voughts, but they were coming for us fast. The *federales* knew that Cedillo was bringing in aircraft and probably were on patrol to intercept any ship from the north. I put the Travelair into a quick, tight power loop, so fast and small that even if Rebecca had worn no seat belt she couldn't have fallen out. The Mexican ships pulled out of their dive and started to turn away. They didn't like the looks of that loop, and they probably didn't like the looks of the Travelair either. She probably looked like a quick death to them, with her clean lines and knife-like wings. They must have thought she was well armed and flown by some ace. General Cedillo was known to have some German World War I aces flying for him, and his ships had shot down some Mexican Army planes. They probably thought I would try to get away, for they were three to one. When I didn't run, they must have thought that I was very dangerous. Of course I was helpless and didn't even know how to fly the Travelair as she should be flown.

While all this was going on I had climbed to eleven thousand feet and was headed for San Luis Potosí. The three Voughts turned after us and got back into formation. I had the Speedwing wide open now and she needed no pushing. She was leaving that part of Mexico fast. The Voughts dropped back and soon were far behind.

The red phone light flashed on again. "What do you want?" I answered.

"Who were those ships?" Rebecca wanted to know.

"Just some friends saying hello," I told her.

"Friends, hell!" she said, and hung up the phone.

There were mountains ahead and San Luis was not far now. Soon we saw the smudge of smoke from the smelter's high brick and steel stacks near town, then I could see the haze over the city itself. Then we could see the churches and Cedillo's new airport with its brick shops and officers' quarters and the round, castellated towers for the guards in the brick wall around the field. Feeling good, I took a big drink of rum, shoved the prop in low pitch, and looped the Travelair three times over the center of the field. Mechanics, soldiers, and officers ran out of the hangars and hightailed for machine gun positions. I made a long turn and came in. I was getting used to her ways and made a good landing. Some officers drove up in a car and we climbed in. "Here is a ship for the general," I said. "Can you take me to him?"

The general gave me a big *abrazo* and asked how the trip had been. "Fine, fine!" I told him and introduced him to Rebecca. We spent the night in the Governor's Palace and next day toured the town. In the afternoon we went out to the army headquarters with the general and watched a lot of rifle and pistol practice and had a nice barbecue dinner. Rebecca asked me why two cars of soldiers always drove ahead of the general and two more drove behind.

"That is just an old Spanish custom," I said. "There are some very narrow-minded people who wish to shoot my general. They often mine the road with dynamite so they can blow him up. Those cars are to try to save him."

She said, "Oh! And those friends of yours in those three biplanes—they were not friends?"

I said, "No, they also were some people who don't like the general very much."

The general was sitting beside us in the back seat of a big seven-passenger Packard limousine. Understanding most of what was said, he looked at me and laughed. Next day the general gave me a certified check on the Chase National Bank of New York for fifteen thousand dollars, then said, "Captain, when are you going to bring me some more airplanes? The one you have just brought is the best ship we have, so my German pilots tell me. Have you seen the ship today? She has her guns mounted now. They are removing the instruments and closing up the front seat, and painting on my colors and identification. Tomorrow, if you wish, you may test her. Maybe you can find your three friends in the air someplace.

Rebecca looked at me, her eyes as big as dollars. She said, "You stay out of that ship! They will shoot you down, and how will I get home?" The old general laughed.

Next day they flew us north in a new Spartan civilian job and landed us in the Sierra Madre. From there we went by mule down into Sonora and got on El Rápido for Nogales.

When Rebecca arrived at her own airport, she was tired and dirty and travel-worn; but she was happy, for she was over four thousand dollars ahead in cash money. She loved money and adventure, and this sort of aircraft business looked like big stuff to her. She was worried about what Washington was going to say when there was no Speedwing, only papers. But the day of reckoning was still far off; she was a millionaire anyway and had her father's attorneys to help her, so what the hell. Her many admirers, boy friends, and other hangers-on all wanted to know where she had been for the better part of a month, but she didn't give them much satisfaction. Her admirers included doctors, lawyers, pilots, cattlemen, oilmen, some plain bums, and playboys, all wanting to get in on her millions. Her having gone off with a vagabond flyer who was a known *contrabandista* and a wild maverick really nettled them.

A few of her "important" friends came and asked her what she was doing, going off for long periods of time alone with me. She told them that she was over twenty-one, earning and spending her own money, and just what the hell was it to them? This made it look like a love affair, so they came to me and said that I should straighten up, marry the girl, and help her with her growing aircraft business and stop prospecting and all the other damn fool things I did.

I said, "Marry her yourself! What do I want with a wife? I have three wives now and five other women pregnant that I know of. Take care of your own damn business and I will try to take care of mine!" They withdrew, shaking their heads.

After about a week, Rebecca began phoning airports around the country and let it be known that she wanted another Speedwing, but no good ones were for sale. People thought she was getting ready for the Powder Puff Derby or going to try for some new records to go with one she already held.

I often went to her big home to eat, at any time of day I was hungry, or to use the long distance phone; She could not conduct this contraband work from her office because of her nosey employees. I drove her big Duesenberg around town and to her field and enjoyed the dirty looks I got from her following who thought I, like themselves, was out for her money. The truth is, I was afraid of her big money. She was the last woman in the world I would marry. Too damn dangerous. I wouldn't dare go to sleep around a woman like that.

At last we bought two nice ships, a Waco taperwing with a 180-horsepower Hisso engine, a very famous ship that had won some races and had been owned by a famous woman flyer. The other ship was a single engine Ford—a good, all metal transport that looked like a Ford Trimotor but was smaller and carried one 3-5 Wright engine, a Navy Wright rated at 220-horsepower. She was clean, with a factory-rebuilt engine, and looked like new. This little single engine Ford was a fine light transport, good for short and rough fields. She also was good for landing in deep brush, with her high wings and lots of prop clearance. Like all Fords, she had corrugated aluminum skin and was good for a light bomber or for light cargo work. General Cedillo needed such ships badly. The new Spartans he had were faster than this Ford, but not as tough; she could really take it.

One day I arrived at Rebecca's mansion on the large estate near the city. Her mother always treated me as a son. She spoke with an accent and was a very sweet old lady. She knew that her daughter was wild about airplanes and that planes were dangerous, but there was no holding Rebecca. She had seen her return from many long and dangerous trips with me; she also had seen her business grow and prosper, and, gave me some of the credit. She also knew that I had never tried to take her daughter for any money and considered me a family friend. Rebecca was afraid of her mother and obeyed her—up to a point. On this cold morning I entered the big house and a servant showed me to the big parlor. There sat Rebecca's mother, sewing.

"Good morning, Captain," she said. "Sit down and Rebecca will be here shortly." Then she sent for some Jewish bread, fresh from the family oven. When Rebecca arrived her mother said, "Rebecca, bring some of Papa's best whiskey for him."

"No," said Rebecca, "he gets no whiskey; we are flying today."

"Rebecca! Bring Papa's best whiskey here at once! And hurry, do you hear?"

"Yes, mother," she said, glaring at me.

So I talked with Rebecca's mother and drank glass after glass of the fine whiskey and soda and ate the good bread while Rebecca ground her teeth and cursed under her breath.

Her mother said, "Now, Captain, take care of my daughter, do you hear? Don't fly too fast and high. And this time see that she brings her coat back with her. She left her coat in

Mexico the last trip. Rebecca, open another bottle of Papa's whiskey. Rebecca! Do you hear?"

Rebecca answered very low, "Yes, mama." She was so mad she didn't trust her own voice.

Poor lady, I thought. Left her damn coat in Mexico. We were lucky not to have left our lives in Mexico. Poor lady, if you only knew.

I took one more water glass of 25-year-old Irish potato whiskey and shoved a couple of chunks of the bread into the pocket of my leather airmail pilot coat. "All right, copilot! Let's go! Let's fly the wings off of them," I said to Rebecca. Outside, by the big side carriage entrance, stood one of the family Pierce-Arrow limousines with a chauffeur. He opened the back door and smiled at me. The family knew that I held her life in my hands and that I was doing what I could to keep her alive, so I stood ace-high with their servants and household. They all knew her and didn't envy my job.

"Now," she said on the Pierce's telephone to the driver, "take us to Kansas City. And use the whip!"

"But, ma'am, Kansas City is over three hundred miles!"

"I didn't ask how damn far it is to Kansas City, get this crate of castings out on the main line!"

He nodded and hung up the phone. The gravel flew as the big Pierce-Arrow stepped out and down the long driveway to the highway. She handed me a package and said, "Here are the engine and airplane logs on the Waco I bought at Kansas City. The Hisso engine is new; only five hours' ferry time on it. The ship has just been rebuilt by Charlie Babb. She should suit the general. The Hisso has gun synchronizers so he may mount guns and shoot through the propeller."

In Kansas City we sent the Pierce-Arrow back. We spent the night in a small hotel and left at daybreak in the Waco for Fort Worth, where we picked up the little Ford. She flew

the Ford and I flew the Waco to Fort Stockton, Texas, where
we gassed up for the last time and beat it south. The taperwing Waco could fly rings around the Ford, but I throttled
the good old Hisso back to save gas, because this time we
didn't have enough in the Waco to reach San Luis. In the
Ford we had a fifty-five-gallon drum of gas so we could fill
up both ships, or at least add enough extra gas somewhere in
Mexico to make San Luis. The Ford had a large cargo door
and the drum entered the cabin very nicely after we had removed a few seats. We didn't dare go near any airports in
Mexico, as the *federales* were watching for strange ships. The
revolution had not really started yet, but people were ex-
pecting it to explode any day. The *federales* were looking for
Cedillo's ships all the time, hoping to shoot them down.

We crossed the border into Mexico just south of the Santi-
ago Mountains and were over Coahuila. All was desert beneath us, with a small rancho here and there. We dropped to
about five thousand feet and made good time. The Waco had
a small pump to transfer fuel from her big fuselage tank to
the center section tank, and from there the gas was gravity-
fed to the big Stromberg carburetor between the Hisso's cylin-
der banks. This little pump was air-driven by a little prop,
and the entire pump assembly sat out in the slipstream. There
was a glass tube beneath the center section in which the pilot
could see the gas moving if the pump was working properly.
I tried this little pump out before we crossed the border, and
it was working okay then. Now I needed gas but could see
nothing in the glass tube. I tried to prime the little pump by
hand but could not get it to deliver. All this time the big
Hisso was eating up gas, and the marker ball in the guage
below the tank was getting near bottom. I flew close to the
Ford, pointed down, and started looking for a clear place to
land.

We were now well into Mexico and not far from Concepción del Oro, a gold mining town in the state of Zacatecas. There were rolling hills below us and some rough looking arroyos, but there also were a few large playas. We went in and set down on one of those old dry lake beds. I landed first. The hot Waco burned the clay as she touched, then tried to ground-loop, as Wacos always did, but at last she stopped with the Hisso engine idling nicely. I cut the ignition and climbed down.

The Ford came in, two-pointed and bounced, and her right landing wheel came off. There was a screech of aluminum on the clay as the engine dug into the dry lake, and she rolled slowly over on her back like a dead dragon fly. Dust rose, and smoke boiled up as oil and gas poured onto the hot engine. Out of the crushed cockpit came Rebecca, spitting blood and teeth.

"Run!" I shouted, "Run, you damn fool! She may flame up any second!" Instead of running away from the wrecked ship, she went back into the cabin for the fire extinguisher and her big purse.

The ship didn't burn, so we rolled the heavy gas drum out of the cabin and over to the Waco. Rebecca started filling my center section tank with buckets, using a big funnel with a chamois for a filter. She had to siphon the gas from the drum into the bucket, then climb up to the high center-section tank and filter the gas into the ship. I took the gas transferring pump apart, but found that it was okay. I then checked the suction line and found it plugged with bits of playing cards. The strainer screen had been removed to allow the paper to clog the line. Somebody probably had fixed it up for the former owner, because no one had known that we were going to buy the ship. After some hours of flying, the pieces of playing cards had plugged the line completely.

I cleaned the line, losing a lot of gasoline on the ground, but we had the full drum to make it up. After filling all tanks and adding two quarts of oil, I hand-cranked the Hisso while Rebecca took care of the throttle and brakes. Then I touched a match to the Ford and ran back to the Waco as the Ford became a roaring furnace.

I had acted none too soon, for on the edge of the playa appeared about twenty-five mounted men, riding toward us. They looked like vaqueros, and probably were, but they may have been a troop of *rurales*. We didn't know whose side they were on, but we soon found out they didn't like us. Rebecca was now in the front seat of the Waco, and I climbed into the back cockpit, jerking on my helmet and goggles. The horsemen were still a long distance away, but they stopped, dismounted, and started shooting at us with rifles. A slug went through the rudder with a zing. Another ripped the center-section gas tank. Some more went through the upper wing. Gas started to pour out of the tank, and the idling prop blew it back all over Rebecca and the whole plane.

I said, "Quick, goddammit, jam your handkerchief into the bullet hole! Do you want us to burn to death?" She stood up in the front seat and tried to get her handkerchief into the hole, but she could not reach the tank through the small bullet hole in the fuselage. Then I said, "Rebecca, you had better go back to the Ford and get your new coat; remember what your mother said before we left."

Her eyes flashed and she snarled, "You son of a bitch!"

I always carry a big machete in my ship, stuck down by the frame and tied with a silk thread, right next to the seat. The silk breaks easy, and a man can get the machete clear to fight with it or cut his way out of a wreck—or cut some other poor bastard out. I grabbed it now and cut a hell of a gash in the rear of the center section so Rebecca could reach the tank. Fabric, wood, and metal of the trailing edge were cut away. Rebecca plugged the hole in the tank with her neck scarf, jamming it in with the handle of a pair of pliers. The horse-

MANUEL

men, having remounted, were coming fast and shooting from the saddle, but we were ready to go, and I poured on the coal. We were airborne at once, and soon were safe from the horsemen. I looked down and saw them below us on the big white playa, gathered in a big circle around the burning Ford, still shooting at us; but the ship was eating up the miles, and the bullets were short. We were on our way to the general's stronghold, with the ripped center-section covering flapping in the wind.

From Concepción del Oro to San Luis Potosí is less than 175 miles by air, and we were soon there. We landed safely on General Cedillo's airfield. The general himself came out to look the Waco over and saw the bullet holes and the gas leaking a little through the silk scarf.

"Well done, *capitán*," he said. "Who shot at you?" I told him that it was some of his good friends.

"My friends? Where were you, anyway?"

When we told him, he laughed and said, "You are lucky— *very* lucky. If those men catch pilots, they cut off their heads with their helmets and goggles on them and send the heads to us to scare my pilots. Whenever my pilots catch mounted troops out in the open, they give them hell, so it goes hard with pilots if they fall into their hands."

While we were eating, the general talked about the many ships he needed, and Rebecca said she would send them as fast as she could find good ones. He had a number of sources for aircraft, but few were getting through to him. He paid Rebecca in full for both ships, saying he would count the Ford as lost in combat.

We were once more flown in a new Spartan into the Sierra Madre and from there made our way to Mazatlán, Sinaloa, where we took a small boat to Ensenada, Baja California. It was a little beatup Mexican steamer that traded along the coast, and we had quite a voyage. We took one more ship to

General Cedillo, a big Travelair 6000 with a new engine. We had no trouble on this trip, as we flew high and nonstop. We carried two full drums of gas in the cabin and a hand-wabble pump to transfer gas to the tanks in flight. Rebecca received her pay from the general, and I received my expenses from both the general and Rebecca. Everyone has to pay me expenses when I am on a dangerous job. On the last trip, we left from Tampico, in a small Mexican fishing boat, which set us ashore in the Laguna Madre. We then made our way on rented mules to Matamoros.

Soon after our last trip the revolution started. General Cedillo eventually was defeated and was hiding out in an old mine tunnel in the mountains of Michoacán when he was shot by a man who later became governor of Nuevo León.

15

Adventure in Honduras

AFTER GENERAL CEDILLO WAS SHOT DOWN, things got quiet once more in Mexico. I was doing some prospecting in Sonora. Having married my Yaqui wife, Puñalita, I started cashing in big on gold. One time I landed at Rebecca's new airport sporting a good airplane and gold in my pockets. I was throwing money around like water and paying no taxes, and all this made Rebecca's mouth water.

"Take me with you," she said. "I want to see some of those mines of yours. We never had time to stop when you took me before, but now we can look around and see things." She could talk sweet when she smelled a gold mine. "Let's go now, back to old Mexico! I heard you were in Honduras and other places in Central America. What were you doing?"

I avoided a direct answer, and the conversation turned to the weather. Was it hot in Honduras? she wanted to know. I said that it was *very* hot the day I left, and also hazy. "Like the time you broke up poor old General Cedillo's Ford on the playa, there was a lot of haze caused by flying lead." Then I asked her if she knew where I might buy a good Ford Trimotor ready to go. In this day there were still a few Fords flying around in the U.S.A. The Grand Canyon Air Lines, out of Tucson, had one and there were several others here and there.

"Yes," she said, "I know of a Ford in Des Moines, Iowa. It belongs to a flower company there and they want five thousand dollars cash for it. Do you have that much money?"

"Yes," I said, "I've got that much money, right here in my flying coat."

"What do you want with a Ford, anyway?" She pressed. "You have a nice ship right there in that Ryan you are flying."

Finally, I told her. I needed it to haul some mining machinery—a five-stamp mill, a Pelton waterwheel, some pulleys, shafting, and other equipment for milling some highgrade freemilling ore.

After a string of other questions, she said, "Goddammit, I'm sick and tired of this city life. I want to get out again. You know, I haven't had any fun since you and I flew for the general."

So I said, "Why don't you get married, Rebecca? You need a good husband. You should settle down and raise a family now. That cattleman from Texas would be a good man for you, latch on to him; he looks like he could take a good beating."

She just said, "Oh, you son of a bitch!"

At last she told me that she wanted to go prospecting and mining and that she also wanted to see Central America. "Let

me into this stamp-mill deal of yours. I want to learn something about mining machinery. Won't you teach me?"

I said I would teach her what little I knew, but I didn't
want any more partners in this deal, for it wasn't big enough
for more than the three of us now in it. I had my partners
already, including a Honduran general. She wanted to know
all about it, and I told her.

"We have old Spanish workings that our prospector found
away back in the interior. A long tunnel runs into a big
quartz vein on the side of a deep cañon. When the old man
found the workings, he was following up some placer gold
on a little river called the Río Coco. This river flows into the
ocean at Cape Gracias á Dios. He was far up the river on a
small tributary that has no name, tracing the placer gold up
this stream, when he came upon a very old mine dump,
covered with brush. Big ferns and trees a hundred years old
or more were growing out of it. This gold mine is probably in
Nicaragua, but we don't know for sure. The maps of this
country are no good. It is very near the border.

"The prospector went into the old tunnel above the dump
and a big yellow *tigre* ran out, brushed past him, and dashed
away into the thick jungle. The vein carries a lot of gold. You
can see the gold in the quartz with the naked eye, and the
vein is from three to four feet wide. It is in the wildest part
of the country, in deep rain forest. There are no roads and no
maps.

"The general can fix it up for us to work the mine. We
have made an airstrip in the jungle, and not far from the
mine—by air—we have this stamp mill that we bought in
Honduras, with the water wheel and everything else we will
need. The fall of the river will turn the stamp mill, and we
will crush the ore at almost no cost. The rock is freemilling
and most of the gold can be caught on copper plates and

blankets. With a shaking table thrown into the flow sheet, I believe we have it made."

"My!" she said. "That sure sounds like a good deal. Take me with you on just this one trip. I'll pay all expenses and work too. I want to see some more of the south."

"Well," I said, "you are troublesome and mean; also a woman is bad luck around a mine, and the general says . . . ."

"I don't care what the general says!" she yelled. "Take me with you; I'll help you."

"You can't leave a big layout like this, can you Rebecca? Not like you used to, I'm sure."

"Can't I? I'll show you how quick I can leave. Watch this." She gave a few orders to a couple of her office people and picked up her flying coat and said, "Well, what's holding us? I have order in my business. I run my company like a general runs his troops. Let's get your Ryan and get going."

Within the next few days we bought the Ford Trimotor in Des Moines, sold my little Ryan, and were on our way south with a clearance into Honduras from the general in Tegucigalpa. We crossed into Mexico at Brownsville, Texas, on tourist passports and a Mexican clearance for the Ford as a private ship. This was a good Ford. She had three 3-6-9 Wright engines with controllable-pitch Hamilton Standard props, extra large wheels, and a big air wheel on her tail. She had foot brakes instead of the one tall brake lever that was factory equipment. At Des Moines we had taken all the radio out of her and given it away. Radio is just junk. I am my own boss and make my own mistakes and don't need any help from the ground. Radio will get a man depending on it and then go out. Then you *are* in a fix. Without radio you don't go into stuff you might go into otherwise. Blind flight instruments are fine if they are good, but blind flying in jungle and mountains is dangerous. Airline blind flight is one thing and a damn prospector trying to fly blind is another. We always get our flying done before noon in the tropics, with no night flying. So we got rid of the radio and a lot of weight and threw all the cabin seats away. We were going to use the Ford for cargo, and we needed no extra seats.

The first day we flew from Brownsville, Texas, to Villahermosa, Tabasco, and gassed up there. The next day we flew across the state of Campeche and part of Quintana Roo and out to the coast near Chetumal, then followed the coast south until we picked up Puerto Barrios, Guatemala. From there it was only a short hop to San Pedro Sula, on the coast of Honduras, where TACA (Transportes Aeros Central Americanos) has a good airport. We landed there and showed the general's letter to the chief of customs and immigration officials. They gave us papers for the Ford for twenty dollars American, and we were in.

There now is a good road from San Pedro Sula to Tegucigalpa, but at that time there was only a fair mule trail. Soon we were at the capital with the general. He had the stamp mill all cleaned up and painted and the shafting ready to set up as soon as we got it on site. We loaded about half of the equipment for the mill and tied it down good. I had the Ford at Toncantín, TACA's airport south of Tegucigalpa. It is a big field and a good one, and there we loaded and gassed up. Then we headed for the mine. Our strip was about 135 miles east and a little south of Tegucigalpa.

With the old prospector showing the way, it took the general two weeks to get there by boat. They went from La Ceiba clear around to the mouth of the Río Coco in a small fishing boat, up the river in a *cayuco*, then on foot to the mine. It took only a little more than an hour and a half to get to the mine in the Ford. We moved everything for the mill and the camp in three loads. The Ford had easily paid for herself by now and TACA wanted to buy her. TACA had a large shop flew on a TACA plane to Tegucigalpa and found the general. He felt very badly about losing the Ford, but realized we uld have been killed. We were very glad to be alive, although we never found the two Indians. I'm sure the *tigres* t them and the beef.

Rebecca flew back to the States and her business on Pan merican, and later I went home to my Puñalita and the od gold mines I had in Sonora. I needed another ship to go with our gold mine and mill and also some more money. nora was the best place for me just then, as gold came easy r me there. I didn't need any more gold mines anyhow; I d all I could take care of, if I had only had the sense to stay ere and work them.

The old prospector went on working La Cueva del Tigre ine, and I left for Mexico. I was sick for a year, but the arm Sonora sun and the herb teas of the Yaqui witch doc rs fixed me up. My lips got rotten, so I held them over the eam vent of a small hot mineral spring. The steam softened em up and they healed with but a few small scars.

I have often wondered how the mine came out, but have ever gone back. Other matters came up, and from Sonora I ent to South America.

at Toncantín and operated ten or twelve Fords on cargo jobs all over Central America. It also had an extensive passenger airline service using Fords, Bellancas, and other ships. The Rosario and the Agua Fría gold mines depended on TACA for transportation of almost everything they needed to operate. TACA developed and built the first air oil tankers at Toncantín, using Ford Trimotor ships. On the heavy cargo ships they had a heavy duralumin I-beam in the cabin roof and handled parts of one-hundred-ton ball mills with heavy chainfalls on this beam. TACA was far ahead of anyone in the world in air cargo work at one time, and its shops developed a lot of aviation firsts.

The general had a rancho on the Bay Islands off the north coast of Honduras, where he raised cattle. He wanted to get some of the fresh meat into the capital to sell and to place in cold storage. There was a good long beach where a ship could land and get off from his ranch. We made two trips, about twenty-eight miles out to sea, to load up meat and fly it to Tegucigalpa. The meat would have spoiled if moved by boat and mule trail to the capital, but the Ford could handle it very well, with no spoilage and at a good profit.

After the second trip we went back up to the mine to see how the old man and the Indians were coming with the mill, and to find out what supplies they would need. When we got back from the mine, the general asked us to make another trip for a load of meat.

Early one morning Rebecca and I and three Indians left for the islands. The Indians were to do the butchering and load the beef, then they would stay on the ranch while two other Indians from the ranch would return with us and the cargo. While the Indians rounded up and butchered the cattle, I went fishing, and Rebecca fooled around exploring the island.

Early next morning, we got off the beach in good shape, but when we got to the mainland shore we ran into heavy rain—very unusual for so early in the day. There was no going above it, and when I tried to turn back, the ceiling was down to the water. I turned inland and flew over the jungle just above the trees, with mountains all around. The rain was so heavy that I could see nothing; water poured into the cockpit and leaked around the windshield. I couldn't find the beach to land and couldn't climb because one outboard engine had drowned out.

Near the equator the storms are small in diameter but violent and turbulent. Small rough storm centers form out at sea or in mountain passes without warning. These cyclones, though small, are pure hell when you run into one. This one probably had swept in from the Caribbean, and the cooler mountains of the coast range had caused it to dump its cargo of warm rain.

We were blind, and the air was rough. Lightning flashed, and sparks and blue fire jumped from different places in the all-metal Ford. There was a great hollow of yellow-blue electricity around the center prop. The air was so full of water that the poor engines either couldn't breathe or the ignition was drowned out. I said to Rebecca, "Go back and throw out everything." Rebecca always obeyed orders under fire. She dashed back among the Indians and the meat. She spoke very little Spanish, but the meat started going overboard through the big cargo doors. Both engines were in low pitch and wide open, but the water was forcing the ship lower and lower. Then the other outboard engine went out, and down we went. With the good old center engine wide open, we crashed nose high into dense jungle. The tail struck first. The ship was nearly stalled and light, now that the meat was gone.

I learned later that the Indians were gone too—jumped out into the jungle, Rebecca said. Maybe she shot them. *¿Quién sabe?* She had a big Frontier model Colt forty-five that the general had given her to carry to the island, with a written

permit to shoot anybody she saw fit. I couldn't have shot back in the cabin in all that storm.

The prop dug into the big trees, and the last I rem seeing the sticks and leaves fly as I cut the ignition. thing I heard was water running. When I opened the storm had gone inland and the sun was shining The deep jungle was steaming. The water I heard was a little stream nearby. A big *guacamaya* [mac slowly flying by.

High above me in the big trees was the Ford, on but still held by the branches. I don't know how I hurt all over and my face was covered with blood. was smashed and cut, and I could not see very we by Rebecca showed up and said there was a trail n and she would follow it to the coast. She wanted to badly I was hurt.

"Hell," I said, "I do not know how bad I am hur seen my lawyer yet!" I asked her where the Indi

"They jumped," she said. "When the meat we just jumped after it. I couldn't stop them."

Well, there were more important things to than a couple of Limpieras that didn't know an to jump out of low flying airplanes.

I told Rebecca, "Goddammit, go up in the shi bottle of Jamaica rum and the serapes, it is cold the ground. And while you are at it, get your co coat, and you remember what your mother sa sure and see she doesn't lose her coat.' "

She climbed up into the broken branches a down with two serapes and the rum. I man drink, and she covered me with the serapes. Af came back with some Indian fishermen and a s they got me to the coast. It was a couple of w could catch a small fishing boat going to La Ce

Epilogue

THE START OF WORLD WAR II in Europe found El Lobo flying for a little tropical airline in Central America, making "good money" on diamonds and other jewels coming into Panama with Jewish refugees from Hitler's Germany. By bartering their jewels, the refugees often were able to get where they wanted to go and perhaps establish themselves in a new home. By knowing what palms to grease, El Lobo was able to slash red tape for these unfortunates, but he did not do such favors gratis.

"I made so much money I couldn't carry it all around with me," he said. Like many persons in Latin America, he did not believe in banks. He had a habit of leaving money with bartenders in towns scattered over several small republics for safekeeping.

When the Japanese bombed Pearl Harbor and the United States entered the war, he was in Panama. "I was not mad at anybody," he recalled, "and decided to let them fight it out among themselves. The only wars I care about are little revolutions where you get paid well for fighting and flying and, if you are on the winning side, maybe get a ranch for a present, like I did in Nyarit."

He was about ready to shuck his job and go prospecting when he was tapped to help the U.S. Army Engineers fly into some of the little jungle fields used by the airline, to set up antiaircraft batteries. But the army way was not his, and the company was putting pressure on him because of his smuggling activities. "They all did as much smuggling as they could," he said, "but I had better contacts and was liberal with my money." Then one day he flew into Tegucigalpa, Honduras, "a little drunk and showing off," and came too close to a hill. The starboard engine of the Ford Trimotor was raked off on a coconut palm tree, and he decided it was time to move on.

Taking up with a group of Indian shark fishermen, he alternated between fishing, beachcombing, and prospecting.

After getting his fill of fishing and beachcombing, he drifted to Panama City, where he had "a good time with the girls and drank lots of rum" until his money played out, then got a job with the Panama Canal as a diesel mechanic and magneto expert and traveled all over the Canal Zone repairing equipment. For recreation he bought a San Blas-rigged *cayuco* (fishing boat) and did a lot of sailing around the bay.

Then he met a Costa Rican girl, who had been lured to Panama with the promise of employment, only to find the job was in a house of prostitution. She was a fisherman's daughter, and they fled together in his *cayuco* after El Lobo helped her satisfy her desire for vengeance by setting fire to the whorehouse in which she had been offered the job.

The girl, revolted at the thought of selling her favors, now exchanged them for passage home to Costa Rica.

El Lobo then went north to the United States and called on Rebecca at her Midwestern headquarters to propose a deal whereby they would purchase aircraft engines for army use in Central America. Greeting him with the news that his mother had died seven years previously, Rebecca urged him to see the family lawyer and settle the estate before beginning their new venture.

"They have been looking everywhere for you," she told him. "Your exwife is trying to get your mother's ranch and a lot of your father's mining property."

"Hell," responded Ricardo, "I don't want anything from my family. I never did anything the family wanted me to do; I told them when I left that I was long gone, so I don't think I've got anything coming. I don't like gringo lawyers, and this is no longer my country. . . . To hell with the estate, let's go!"

Typically, he seemed to draw from a store of knowledge no one suspected that he possessed to find antiquated engines in storage all over the country and move them to California for overhaul before they were shipped to Panama. The government was paying the bills, and he seemed to enjoy the wheeling and dealing he was able to do. "There was a lot of fun on this job," he recalled, "and I think that I did a little bit for the U.S.A. in keeping their Panama Canal defenses going."

When the job was done, the colonel of the Army Engineers commended him and offered him a high recommendation to his next employer. But he said, "No, thanks, I never use them," and faded into the Andes of South America.

I lost track of El Lobo for a number of years, then ran into him in Mexico, D.F., quite unexpectedly. He told me of some of the highlights of his experiences during those years—of shooting up a Communist mob when he and some of his army officer friends, all well armed with Thompson submachine guns, were under attack in a government building. I think this occurred in Chile, but do not recall the exact location or events leading up to it. Knowing him as I did, I am quite sure that all were well lubricated with alcohol.

He also told me of finding an ancient Spanish mine, high in the Andes, in whose extensive workings he found many skeletons of Indian slave miners chained to the wall rock.

He flew for small airlines, carrying everything from passengers to pigs, poultry, cocoa, machinery, and anything else that a plane could get off the ground with in the high-altitude airfields of the Andean countries. Knowing him, I'm sure he also carried various contraband on his own account.

During the 1954 revolution in Guatemala, he flew some of the losing politicians out of the capital under fire. His plane was badly shot up and many passengers were wounded, but he managed to fly it nearly to the Pacific coast before crashing in the jungle. The only survivor, he himself was badly injured. He stayed with the wreck, dressing his injuries as best he could with the first aid kit. When he was able, he went through the passenger baggage, salvaged what he could, and moved upwind from the wreck and the decomposing bodies. There he made a crude camp and nursed his wounds.

He hadn't been paid, and had lost his plane, which may or may not have belonged to him, and, as he always said, everyone paid when he was on a dangerous job; so his conscience, I'm sure, bothered him not in the least as he performed his ghoulish search of the wrecked plane. One of his passengers must have been a high official of the overthrown government, perhaps the treasurer, for El Lobo found a bag crammed full of money—mostly U.S. currency, but also some gold coins.

When he felt strong enough to attempt to walk to the coast, he started off with the bag of money. But he was still in such bad shape that he had to cache the bag. He found a place where it would be protected from the jungle rains and oriented himself so that he might return for it when he was able. He finally made it to the coast, more dead than alive, and remained in critical condition for many months. He was still convalescing when we met again.

Now broke and down on his luck, he was trying to raise funds to return and recover the money before the tropical moisture destroyed it. The currency wouldn't last through many rainy seasons. He offered me half if I would go with him and pay the expenses, but I had lost nothing in that jungle. And I wondered a bit about his being the sole survivor. He may have known about the money. "*¡Los muertos no hablan!*" He had been in the tropics long enough to have small regard for life—his own or anyone else's. In any event, he had been unable to find a sponsor. The old general who had financed many of his escapades in the past had died and there was no one such as he to turn to.

I am no adventurer, having always believed that adventures are apt to be the result of misfortunes spawned by one's own stupidity. Sure, I've had a few close calls and some sad experiences, but I would have been much happier to have avoided them. There was the time, for example, that I came very close to shooting one of my own men. He had been hired in one of the little mountain pueblos as guide and *cargador*. We had just finished our lunch of some surplus K-rations I had purchased in the States, which the men seemed to enjoy greatly. Suddenly, without warning, a knife whizzed past my ear. Narrowly missing me, it stuck, quivering, in the tree beside me. I whirled, drawing my pistol, and had the hammer back when the man who had thrown the knife raised his hands, and, with a sickly grin, said it was all a joke to see if I were *muy hombre*. Some joke, I thought. I made the best of it, for it would have meant a lot of trouble, with my other men and with the authorities, had I pulled the trigger. But I never let that man get behind me again.

Back to El Lobo. Shortly after our meeting in Mexico following his crash, I returned to the States to get my affairs in shape and to obtain the wherewithal to resume prospecting. I had attended closely to my assaying business and consulting

work in Rapid City, South Dakota, for a year or more when I
received a letter from El Lobo. He was in the *cárcel* in Toluca, on a homicide charge of which he swore he was innocent. He told me he had a tremendous fund of information on
old mines, Spanish and revolutionary loot, and hidden Aztec
gold and artifacts. He wanted me to investigate some of these
locations as his equal partner, to help him raise funds for a
new trial or to buy his freedom. I knew that he probably had
more such data filed away in his conniving brain than any
other man alive, for he was a tireless investigator. He was a
bit more prone to pin his faith on old legends told by some
peon in exchange for an evening of pulque or mescal than he
should have been, but much of the information he had was
valid.

Some time later, in July, 1961, I returned to Mexico, rented
a small house in Toluca, and visited him in the prison for several hours on many different days. I was not permitted to take
a recorder into the compound, so had to make notes. Between
my visits he wrote descriptions of many locations and drew
some rough maps. One such location was a cave near Ixtapan
del Oro, where he had found many idols and other ancient Indian artifacts, years before. Having made himself unwelcome
in that pueblo by nearly destroying the little hotel during one
of his bigger-than-life drinking parties, he didn't think it
would ever be healthy for him to go back there. He advised
me not to let anyone know that I knew him. He also warned
me of many large rattlesnakes infesting the cave, saying,
"They won't bother you unless you start trouble. If you kill
one snake the others smell the blood and come out for you."

Some considerable time later, I did follow the map and
found the entrance to the cave, just as he had described it. But
an earthquake had occurred in the meantime, blocking the
passage about forty feet beyond the entrance. I was unable to
investigate many of the locations, as my time was limited,

but I gave him what encouragement I could and promised to return, better financed, in about a year.

A few days before Christmas, somewhat more than a year later, El Lobo phoned me from Mexico. He was out of prison and wanted me to get right down there and help him recover the loot of General Salgado. He had once been to the site alone and had recovered some small portion of the treasure but had been scared off by some Indians. He thought that the recovery could be made safely if we both went, posing as the *gambusinos* we were, established our camp nearby, and were careful to avoid observation. There was a large quantity of silver and gold bars, looted from many mines during the revolution, which Salgado had buried only a few days before he was captured and executed. The recovery of only a small portion of such rich plunder would go far toward refinancing both of us, even after paying the fifty percent required by the Mexican government on finds of treasure trove.

Getting the Jeep ready in short order, I left Rapid City the second day after his call. After driving more than a thousand miles with only a roadside nap, I was so exhausted that I was forced to stay overnight in a Sonora, Texas, motel. When I got to Piedras Negras, across from Eagle Pass, I found that I would be delayed getting through customs with my gear. The *aduana* personnel had a week's Christmas holiday, and I had to leave the loaded Jeep in the compound until the *jefe* returned to give me clearance. There was nothing to do but cool my heels in one of the hotels and get used to Mexican food again until the wheels of government slowly turned. When the holiday had passed, I couldn't complain of any further delay, as the *jefe* remembered me from many previous crossings and knew that I did not carry contraband. I was less than an hour getting my papers fixed up. When one cooperates with customs people and doesn't attempt to smuggle, there is seldom trouble.

When I got to Toluca, having driven the entire distance without rest except an hour or two napping at the roadside, I found that El Lobo had disappeared during the time I was held up at the border.

No one knew where he had gone. The police also were looking for him, as he was out on bond. I made inquiries of all that I thought might have any information as to his whereabouts, but learned nothing except that he had feared for his life and wanted desperately to get out into the *campo*. There were no longer the high prison walls and guards to keep him from his enemies in the city. The secret police probably kept tabs on me, just in case he should try to contact me. It is anyone's guess what happened to him. Possibly agents of one of the countries that wanted him had managed to kidnap him and take him back to their jurisdiction, or even executed him. But it may be that he got away cleanly and melted into the mountains, for he could be a slippery customer when circumstances required it.

I finally gave up and went prospecting with a Mexican friend, mostly looking over prospects that he or his family and friends wanted evaluated. I got most of my expenses in this manner and remained in the pleasant climate of southern Mexico until the worst of the winter weather was over in the north. On the return trip, on the outskirts of Monclova, I saw in the Jeep's headlights two large *tigres* feeding on a cow they had pulled down. They showed absolutely no fear in the glare of the lights and I could have shot them easily but didn't want to risk the sound of shots being heard and the certain delay while my papers were examined. After getting through United States Customs, I went as usual to the Eagle Hotel in Eagle Pass and had a big gringo meal. And as usual it made me ill after having been accustomed to Mexican food.

Among some of the items El Lobo gave me at the prison was a letter, from which the heading had been cut, stating

that since the death of Jimmy Angel, he had been selected as
the "Greatest Adventurer in Aviation." The letter was dated
January 9, 1957, and was signed by V. P. Flynn. Perhaps it
was from an explorer's club or even possibly the old "TTT"
(Typical Tropical Tramps), if that very loose organization
still exists. There also was a photograph of the diesel-powered
yacht he had loaded with Winchesters and ammunition at
the Miami yacht basin, which was sunk, or perhaps shot from
under him, far up the Amazon. Another photograph showed
a bombed-out steamer, a memento of the Guatemalan revolution of 1954-1955. I never learned his connection with this
ship. Perhaps he was the bomber pilot, though he attributed
the bombing to "a friend of mine." There also was a photo of
the old general, El Gordo, bossing some peones who were digging up some of the loot he had buried during the revolution.
El Lobo had taken this picture surreptitiously, for the general
was skittish about having his picture taken in such circumstances. El Lobo had used a Minox, the miniature German
camera so beloved by old cloak-and-dagger people. We used
to call it the "spook camera." It was quite expensive and hard
to come by outside of government purchase for many years.

These tales of a few of the adventures and misadventures
of a most fabulous character may read like the product of an
overactive imagination, but they are real. El Lobo himself
was a master storyteller, with the gift of total recall and a fa-
cility for drawing word pictures. I have tried to recapture his
way of speaking and to tell these stories in his own words as
nearly as possible. Much that he told me has been corroborat-
ed by our mutual acquaintances.

He seemed to enjoy getting himself into bizarre and often
dangerous situations. His ideal of a proper sort of man was a
combination of Lee Christmas—the famous North American
revolutionist who once held Guatemala—Richard Hallibur-

ton, and Errol Flynn. Why he chose me for a friend and confidant has long puzzled me. We were opposites, for he was a big man, well over six feet tall, well-proportioned and quite strong physically, while I am a little guy. He was a hard drinker, while I seldom touch alcohol. While he never smoked, I am a heavy smoker. About the only things we had in common were admiration for beautiful women and an obsession for exploration, especially of old Spanish mines and the mines and towns destroyed during the revolution. We both loved to explore pre-Columbian ruins and look for artifacts that might yield a clue to the life of those ancient civilizations.

Why did he choose me to write these episodes of his life? Many years ago I wrote and published a miners' and prospectors' newsletter. He liked the way I wrote, and he probably didn't know any other writer who understood mining and prospecting—one he trusted, anyhow.

There are few of us still around who knew him well. The old generals of the revolution are gone. World War II ended an era, and El Lobo himself was just about the last of the old breed of "Typical Tropical Tramp." His type—if such a person can be typed—was born with an obsession to see the other side of the mountain. Some may consider them the breed of the damned, for they appeared on the surface to live their lives only for themselves. But in truth, their friendship and trust were precious to hold. In each of them was a little of Don Quixote.

References to Notes

PART ONE

Acosta, Roberto. *Apuntes Históricos Sonorenses: La Conquista Temporal y Espiritual del Yaqui y del Mayo*. Mexico: Imprenta Aldina, 1949.

Bannon, John Francis, ed. *Bolton and the Spanish Borderlands*. Norman: University of Oklahoma Press, 1964.

Brinckerhoff, Sidney B., and Odie B. Faulk. *Lancers for the King: A Study of the Frontier Military System of Northern New Spain, with a Translation of the Royal Regulations of 1772*. Phoenix: Arizona Historical Foundation, 1965.

Chidsey, Donald Barr. *The California Gold Rush*. New York: Crown Publishers, 1968.

Fabila, Alfonso. *Los Indios Yaquis de Sonora*. Mexico: Secretaría de Educación Pública, 1945.

Giddings, Ruth Warner. *Yaqui Myths and Legends*. Tucson: University of Arizona (Anthropological Papers No. 2), 1959.

Kinnaird, Lawrence, ed. *The Frontiers of New Spain: Nicolás de Lafora's Description, 1766-1768*. Berkeley, California: The Quivira Society, 1958.

Rolle, Andrew F. *California: A History*. New York: Thomas Y. Crowell, 1963.

Spicer, Edward H. "Northwest Mexico: Introduction," in Robert

Wauchope, ed., *Handbook of Middle American Indians*, VIII. Austin: University of Texas Press, 1969.

PART TWO

Brenner, Anita. *The Wind That Swept Mexico: The History of the Mexican Revolution of 1910-1942*. Austin: University of Texas Press, 1971.

Cockcroft, James D. *Intellectual Precursors of the Mexican Revolution, 1900-1913*. Austin: University of Texas Press, 1968.

Dulles, John W.F. *Yesterday in Mexico: A Chronicle of the Revolution, 1919-1936*. Austin: University of Texas Press, 1961.

Plenn, J. H.: *Mexico Marches*. New York: Bobbs-Merrill, 1939.

Rojas, Alfonso Villa. "Maya Lowlands: The Chontal, Chol, and Kekchi," in Robert Wauchope, ed., *Handbook of Middle American Indians*, VII. Austin: University of Texas Press, 1969.

Vogt, Evon Z. "The Chiapas Highlands," in Robert Wauchope, ed., *Handbook of Middle American Indians*, VII. Austin: University of Texas Press, 1969.

PART THREE

Kinnaird, Lawrence, ed. *The Frontiers of New Spain: Nicolás de Lafora's Description, 1766-1768*. Berkeley, California: The Quivira Society, 1958.

Moorhead, Max L. *The Apache Frontier: Jacobo Ugarte and Spanish-Indian Relations in Northern New Spain, 1769-1791*. Norman: University of Oklahoma Press, 1968.

Owen, Roger C. "Contemporary Ethnography in Baja California, Mexico," in Robert Wauchope. ed.. *Handbook of Middle American Indians*, VIII. Austin: University of Texas Press, 1969.

Spicer, Edward H. "Northwest Mexico: Introduction," in Robert Wauchope, ed., *Handbook of Middle American Indians*, VIII. Austin: University of Texas Press, 1969.

————. "The Yaqui and Mayo," in Robert Wauchope, ed., *Handbook of Middle American Indians*, VIII. Austin: University of Texas Press, 1969.

El Lobo and Spanish Gold, the fourth book produced by Madrona Press, has been printed on Warren's Olde Style white wove, a paper manufactured for long life. Type used for text is eleven-point Waverley with two-point leading, set on Intertype by G & S Typesetters, Austin. Printing by offset lithography was done by Capital Printing Company of Austin, binding by Universal Bookbindery, Inc., of San Antonio.

Design by William A. Seymour

MADRONA PRESS, INC.

AUSTIN, TEXAS

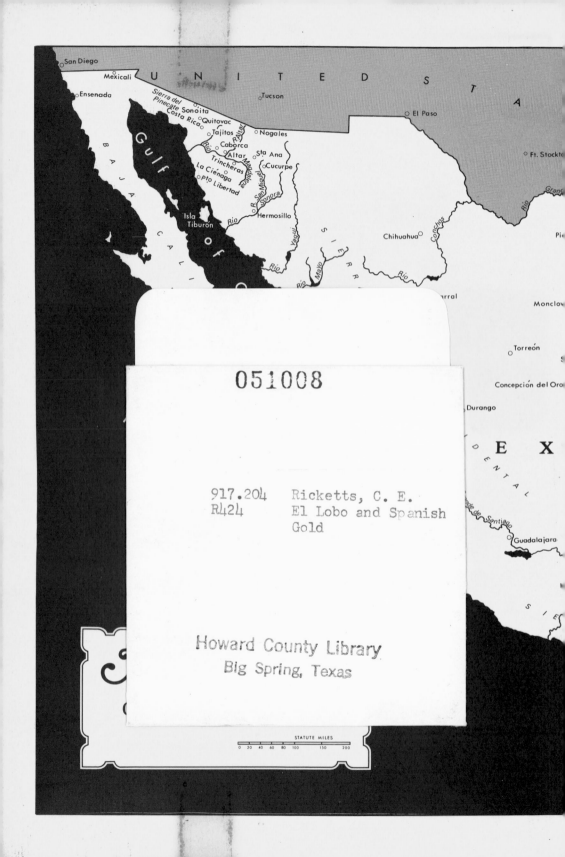